Watchword

Watchword

Pura López Colomé

TRANSLATED BY FORREST GANDER

Wesleyan University Press

Middletown, Connecticut

Wesleyan Poetry

Wesleyan University Press
Middletown CT 06459
www.wesleyan.edu/wespress

Wesleyan University Press is a member of the Green Press Initiative.
The paper used in this book meets their minimum requirement
for recycled paper.

Library of Congress Cataloging-in-Publication Data
López Colomé, Pura, 1952–
[Santo y seña. English]
Watchword / López Colomé; translated by Forrest Gander.
p. cm.
Text in English and Spanish.
ISBN 978-0-8195-7118-2 (cloth : alk. paper)
I. Gander, Forrest, 1956– II. Title.
PQ7298.22.O56715S2613   2011
861'.64—dc23   2011038188

5 4 3 2 1

This project is supported in part by an award from the
National Endowment for the Arts.

NATIONAL
ENDOWMENT
FOR THE ARTS

FRONTISPIECE PHOTOGRAPH: Nina Subin

Ninguna ley podría existir
al fondo de mi estanque cerebral.
Sólo una imago mundi
inconexa, borrosa, vítrea.

No law could exist
in the deep case of my cranium.
Only this imago mundi
disconnected, blurry, vitreous.

Índice

Contents

III. Arborescencias

III. Arborescences

Translator's Preface

How to write about the intimate, the deeply personal, the body, without resorting to confession or to the kinds of detail that can seem almost pornographic? In her newest book, *Santo y seña*, Mexican poet Pura López Colomé writes her best poetry in a style which is less a refinement of how she wrote previously than a condensation of it. The title of her collection gives us a clue to reading the poems. While *santo* means "saint" and *seña* means "sign," the phrase *santo y seña* means "shibboleth" or "watchword." So something important may be hidden, but key words will give us access. What comes clear to the reader quickly enough is that this isn't a literary game, nor even a means of self-protection for the author, so much as it is a mode of perceiving and experiencing trauma and love. The poems are fierce and unapologetically earnest in their wrestling with ontological questions.

Take, for instance, the poem "Tormented." It reminds me of that unforgettable Fra Angelico fresco of Saint Dominic as he concentrates on reading an open Bible while, all around him, Hell's winged demons whirl through the air. Pura's poem begins with objects falling through the air. Not demons, but "solids." It is a more abstract nightmare that nevertheless provokes trembling and "an inky taste" in the mouth. The following phrase, *en su punto* means "on point," literally. But Mexicans use the phrase to indicate something like "all ready" or "just right." When something is set to go, you might say, *Esta en su punto.* Is the inky taste an indication that the speaker is hungry to write? Other watchwords in the poem lead me to think of the bitter aftertaste of chemotherapy. In which case *en su punto* suggests a heightened attentiveness to what might come next.

Like "King Lear," "Tormented" is absorbed with what doesn't come to pass, with *nothing*. Hail doesn't bury the speaker. Monsters don't show up. Distances, brutalities, those sorts of things are notable only by their absence. So why does the poet say that she's left with "Only the agony of acorns"? What's so agonizing about acorns?

Acorns, like little cancer cells. Cells that transform one kind of forest into another. The force of the poem remains implicit. Its very lack of certainty, emphasized by the stop-and-go phrasing, matches the psychological state of the speaker. And the isolated last line, double-spaced below the rest of the poem, turns an ordinary stanza break into an act of metastasis.

Translation's gift is a strange one. It is often, at its best, the gift of strangeness. Pura López Colomé's poetry isn't familiar to us, and not only because we may not have encountered it earlier. Rigorous conceptually and linguistically, it is distinctive from the work of her Mexican peers in its spiritual intensity and its twining of the sacred and profane. The emotional power of the poems is modulated by an unusually high level of (at times kabbalistic) language play and hermeticism—a fact that invites comparisons of López Colomé's poems to those of the incendiary and brilliant seventeenth-century Mexican poet and nun, Sor Juana de la Cruz. A first encounter with either's work can be mystifying, even baffling, which is a good beginning. I remember the art critic Peter Schjeldahl quoting Ed Ruscha's rule: "Bad art is 'Wow! Huh?' Good art is 'Huh? Wow!'" *Watchword*'s poems are of the second category.

In some ways, these poems are highly personal. *Watchword*, which won "Mexico's Pulitzer," the Villaurrutia Prize, in 2007, was written during a bleak period during which the author, diagnosed with cancer, submitted to sequential operations, radiation treatment, chemotherapy, and later reconstructive surgeries. Her psychological outlook wasn't upbeat. She had suffered cancer earlier, in her adolescence. This biographical information, which Pura reminds us in her afterword, "Ethereal Slipknot," is *least* relative to her poetry, does help orient the English-language reader who comes across poems with medical terms like *fomite* (which is material that transmits infection) or poems titled "Deep Wound" or "Almond" (if the reader also knows that cancer patients often consume bitter almonds therapeutically).

Perhaps the most clearly autobiographical poem is "My Life's Portrait," a poem that takes place in three "paintings." The first, "Woman Against a Green Background," is a portrait of Pura's mother who was, herself, a painter. The second, "Waterworm Against a Blue Background," depicts Pura as a child. And the last, "Girl Against a Dark Background," concerns the long-delayed moment when a painting by Pura's mother, by then deceased, was mysteriously delivered to Pura's house in a black plastic bag. Given her own sensitive state, her haunted memories of her mother, and the symbolism of the black bag (which seems, in the breeze, to be breathing), Pura is almost too terrified to open it. But the poem succeeds whether or not you know any of this background information. The familial connections, the elements of narrative, and the biographical detail are liminal characteristics. This poet is more interested in the way language is posed and disposed, in how musicality and syntactical tensions adjust to *create*, not merely *describe*, emotional situations.

For Pura, the world is experienced through the word; we know the world and offer our accounts of it to each other in language. And this phenomenological insistence takes on mystical dimensions. The poems keep turning their undersides to us, flashing us with their source code— "syllables, diphthongs, hiatus"—and asking us to open up to experience, yes, but also to the *language* of experience—the linguistics of hearing, touching, remembering. The way the poems do this is uncanny, profound, and distinguishes the work of Pura López Colomé from work by other contemporary poets—either in the United States or in Mexico.

Her poetry may seem strange at first. And the first section of this book is the most abstract. But strangeness is just the opening gambit. To read this book is to go through something that leaves a permanent mark on you. "Only the difficult," the great Cuban poet José Lezama Lima reminds us, "is deeply stimulating." Pura López Colomé's poems give voice to a world familiar and odd, wounded and, particularly in the third section, hopeful. In the energy and intensity of her poems and in López Colomé's attitude toward words, we discover both a line of conduct and the source for a richer life.

I

Quién eres, qué

A Barrie Cooke, el más abstracto de los figurativos

En este mundo caminamos / sobre el techo
del infierno, / contemplando las flores. —ISSA

I. EL DEMONIO
Despliega sus alas
sin orlas
sin vuelo
al caminar
al azar
al borde de unos setos
que jamás se han percibido
olido
mucho menos
cultivado,
silvestres, casi;
al descubrir
entre su fuego,
no en aquello
que Ilusión resguarda,
que en esta vida
—esta única—
hay que gozar,
dejarse colmar,
bañar de júbilo
y más júbilo
hasta verlo líquido;
hay que nunca
zaherir
a quien se ama
con igual candencia,
igual flama que llama
a que esas aguas
suelten
el primer hervor
ese único.
Y es tan difícil.

Who Are You; What

To Barrie Cooke, the most abstract of the figuratives

In this world we walk / on the roof
of hell, / gazing at flowers —ISSA

I. THE DEMON
Unfurls his flightless,
fringeless
wings
as he strolls
along
a line of hedges
that had gone unnoticed,
never sniffed
nor even
cultivated before,
all but wild;
and what you see
inside his fire,
undisguised
by Illusion,
is that this life
this only life
must be relished,
allowed to brim
and to wash you through with elation
and more elation
until life liquefies;
never would you
expose
someone you love
to such heat,
even for this vision
of a speaking flame
hissing waters
into their first boil
their only boil.
And so the going is hard.

2. BELLEZA, UNA VERDAD

Y se las ingenia uno
para ubicuo ser
ante umbrales

umbras

certidumbres, reciedumbres, costumbres
abiertas
a la vista.

Por ejemplo,
el decoro, las finezas,
semejantes sutilezas
en absoluto innecesarias
cual palabras que definen
el sonido del amor,

apófisis mastoides,

hueso que vibra
en catarata
cantata
del todo desasida
desencadenada
de sí misma
desbocada

de jilguero.

Por ejemplo,
lo que el hado
en virtud de otra persona
logra en uno.
Mucho más consuelo
que el dolor
o su plural:
el incurable
alivio.

2. BEAUTY, A TRUTH

And so you find a way
to stay present
to thresholds, penumbras

umbras

affirmations, consolations, adaptations
come
clear.

For example,
decorum, finesse,
subtleties
as feckless as the words
used to express
the groans of love,

mastoid apophysis

a bone that throbs
in a cascading
cantata
broken loose
unaffiliated
with itself
regurgitated

from a goldfinch.

Consider, for example,
what fate,
by virtue of someone else,
might draw from you.
By far, more consolation
than grief
or its plural:
incurable
relief.

3. MARCA DE NACIMIENTO

Un toque del pulgar:
la luz y la distancia solas.

Un deslizamiento de las palmas:
el universo intuido
insospechado.

Sus líneas,
senderos
de Fortuna
desprovistos
de Futuro.
Y dicen, y hablan
por los tímpanos:
un paisaje en abundancia,
un ansia de buscar
un agotamiento que, de pronto,
se asome entre colinas
y revele
ese jardín
de huella en huella.

3. BIRTHMARK

The touch of a thumb:
nothing but light and distance.

Palm against palm:
an intuited uncharted
universe.

The palm's lines,
Fortune's
lanes,
devoid
of any Future.
But they say
what they have to say:
full as a landscape,
prodding us to seek
the depletion that
peaks between hills
and reveals
a garden
of signs within signs.

4. ÁNGULO MULTIPLICADO E INVISIBLE
Acaso los sueños.

Desde un fondo
color vino,
color ebria soledad,
desde sus penas fluviales
y sus vados,
emerge un ser humano
femenino y tan mortal,
tan de antemano.

Algunas facciones.
Algunos rasgos
propios
de las lenguas
o el color.

Ocres contra blancos,
cabelleras contra pieles,
peso de la carne
contra lo ligero
de una historia personal,
intrascendente;
acuarelas que arrasan,
lágrimas sin sal.
Y aún así,
aquella historia
querría reblandecerse
al óleo:
ser cuerpo herido
en la entretela
que rasgue y elucide
este subsuelo,
este paraíso.

4. MULTIPLIED AND INVISIBLE ANGLE
Perchance to dream.

From wine-
tinged, desolation-
tinged depths, binges,
from fluvial agonies
and their fords,
a human being emerges
in brushstrokes,
feminine and ever so mortal,
from the start.

Certain features take
shape. Strokes
of idiom
and color.

Ochers against whites,
hair against skin,
her muscular weight
against the lightness
of her personal history,
banal as it is;
evaporating watercolors,
saltless tears.
And even so,
such a history
might be softened
in oils:
that the wounded body
in the canvas
might illuminate and elucidate
this underworld,
this paradise.

Tibuchina

Violáceo viaje
a una matriz
al descubierto.
Dedos vegetales
que se estiran ululando
identidad:
sí,
son los míos,
los que tocan las membranas
más delicadas del ojo
por dentro.
Han dejado ahí un residuo dactilar,
un estanque de círculos
irrepetibles.

Algo avanzó por los arroyos,
los hilos de agua
de mis nervios,
una manera táctil de silbar,
de llamarle a alguien por su nombre

aterciopelado

cubriendo de emociones
su rugoso tronco
sin que,
serpentina,
se enrede,
se enrosque,
se encienda
su fragilidad.

Mas los cielos no se abrieron ni voz atronadora
hizo estremecer tejidos interiores aún más tiernos,

meninges

Tibuchina Flower

A violaceous voyage
toward a womb
of discovery.
Vegetal fingers,
ululating, strum up
an identity:
yes,
they're my own,
and they touch the most
delicate membranes of my eye
from the inside.
There they leave a dactylic residue,
a pool of unique
circles.

Something surges through the channels,
the watery threads
of my nerves,
a tactile whistling,
as though someone had been called by name

velvety

the rough bark flushes
with emotions
but without—
serpentining,
entangling,
encircling,
enlightening—
the fragility of emotion.

And yet, the skies didn't open, no thundering voice
reached even the most sensitive tissue.

meninges

tan susceptibles, tan finitas
tan proclives al aumento,
tan sensibles al misterio.
Tan inflamables y estallables.
Tan puertas de par en par
a la sensualidad de un pensamiento
capaz de darle un vuelco a las entrañas.

Que en ese su instante de tranquilidad,
cuando Equilibrio las sorprende
inermes,
pueden recibir la campanada
que las recorra de punta a punta,
enviar el sonido hasta la campanilla
y un sustantivo llenar,
ahora sí,
la boca de verdad.
Un por fuera
prolongándose sin cielo:

tibuchina

que avisa, sosiega,
se clava y penetra,
eje a colores,
gracia en brote.

Sólo tú sabías el nombre
y lo dijiste:
los pistilos,

memoria

en las papilas,
desprotegidas éstas
de la descarga
del sabor.

so susceptible, so limited,
so given to thickening,
so sensitive to mystery.
So inflammable and explosive.
So thrown open like doors
to the sensuality of a thought
capable of turning the stomach.

In that instant of tranquility,
when Equilibrium catches the membranes
off guard,
they absorb the clanging that
vibrates through them, one end to another,
as sound shimmies down to the uvula,
until at last
a word can fill
the mouth with truth.
The outside
goes on minus its sky:

tibuchina

which teases, appeases,
pierces and fixes me
on its axis of color,
thankfulness in bloom.

Only you knew the name
and spoke it:
pistils

memory

stored in the papillae
unprotected
from the firing
taste buds.

Simple y llana flor silvestre

que alguna vez imaginé,
cuyos pétalos entorné
como a las hojas
de una puerta,
como a mis párpados,
y luego conocí en persona,
echada en el pasto algún domingo,
a los diez años de edad.
Y parecía
dirigirme la palabra.

A simple and common wildflower

I think of now and then
whose petals I opened out
like the leaves
of a door,
like my eyelids,
a flower I feel I met *in person*
lying on the grass one Sunday
when I was ten.
And it seems to me that flower
led me to the word.

Tres escenas lacustres

I. SOMNÍFERA
Creí que no existía
deleite
al pie de la letra.

Mirando el cielo cambiante
recostada en una barca,
mecida en cuna primordial
con nupcial velo de tul
y encaje de mortaja
por la tangible mano
del viento.

Todo lo sabe,
es principio que pronuncia
esto no es barca sino barco,
nave de locos, desquicio
ininterrupto.
Las nubes
desmenuzan
su cabello de ángel;
tras él
un alarido ubicuo
—ven, escóndete aquí, ésta es tu casa—
que quiere ser de, pertenecerle a
un sitio
junto a alguna cordillera
un valle con ríos cual nervaduras
de las hojas cuando impúdicas
muestran el envés
o cuando éste se muestra púdico
en el esquema de un cuerpo
con sus músculos y sus dendritas,
cual pertenencias, mis pertenencias,

Three Lacustrine Scenes

I. SOMNIFEROUS

I didn't believe literal
delight
could exist.

Watching the changeable sky,
lying in a boat
rocked in a primeval cradle—
with my tulle marriage veil
and a lace shroud—
by the living hand
of the wind.

Knowing everything to come,
genesis says
this isn't a ferry, just a rowboat,
a ship of idiots, an endless
craziness.
The angel-hair
of the clouds
dissolves and
from behind
them, a howl
—*quick, hide yourself, here's your home*—
seems to echo from,
pertain to,
some neighboring cordillera,
a valley rivered like the nerve system
of leaves when, without shame,
they bare their undersides
or when the undersides shamefully suggest
the schemata of a body
marked by muscles and dendrites,
pertinences, *what pertains to me,*

mis seres queridos
que comienzan a entumecerse

rumbo a otra parte,
difuntos a quienes mi pulso
mece al vivir
como de aire.

He nacido ahí.
Desfallecido.
No merced a un pescador
que me invitó, hechizando,
a seguir sus pasos sin planta,
sino al verdadero dueño
de ese sueño desnudo de temor:
dejarse arrullar, abandonarse,
observar bien,
observar el azul,
no perderse entre las ansias
de caminar sobre las aguas.

my own body parts
which begin to go numb,

to go haywire,
dying off even as my pulse
tries to pump them with life,
so many huffs of air.

I was born there.
Benighted.
No thanks to the spellbinding
fisherman who called me to follow,
soundlessly, in his steps,
but thanks instead to the actual dreamer
of that dream stripped of its terrors:
that dream of letting go, of being lulled,
of looking clearly,
steadily into the blue
instead of losing myself to the longing
to walk on water.

2. VUELTA EN SÍ

La quilla avanza dibujando
un camino antes oculto.
El aire tiene aún
brecha por abrir
con las guadañas de dos rostros
obstinados en robarle
sus bienes a esta tarde,
una isla bosquecillo
donde las ninfas han jugado
entre resquicios de sombra y sombra.

Ese día quise probarlo todo.
Que el paladar no miente
y los platillos saben.
Pasé sin pensarlo por el puente bajo.
Guardé una gota de su olor.
Sostuve los pesados remos y la caña,
aunque no impulsé la nave ni vi nada
que mordiera aquel anzuelo.
El instante se estiraba,
y yo iba ampliando
el círculo vicioso.

2. COMING TO, AGAIN

The keel advances, carving out
a hitherto hidden road.
The air has yet
to be opened—
by the scythes of two faces
intent on cutting every
sweetness from the afternoon—
onto a small forested island
where nymphs once played
in the slits between one shadow and another.

That day, I wanted to taste it all.
Believing my palette wouldn't deceive me
and I'd know each dish.
With nothing on my mind, I drifted under the low bridge.
A drop of its scent wet me.
I gripped the heavy oars and the pole,
although I couldn't steer or see a thing
that might take the bait.
The instant stretched itself out
while I kept expanding
the cruel circle.

3. CARRUSEL

Tres caballos descendieron la colina
y entraron, suntuosos,
a la diafanidad del río.
Uno
se fue vadeando junto a mí.
A ratos se detenía a beber.
A ratos me miraba fijamente.
Y entre ambos,
un murmullo antiguo,
peregrino.

≈

Tus tres caballos, corceles, garañones.
Con los cascos enterrados en el lodo
y el agua hasta las ancas
acariciándoles el vientre.
Abrevando, pastando
en el ondular de sus siluetas.
Uno, aquél,
el alazán,
con la misma tristeza de la yegua
que mi padre intercambió
por dos tordillos siendo mía,
me sorprendió a la deriva:
en la humedad de nuestros ojos,
crines al aire, hierbas fugaces,
un espacio que concierne
—me, le, nos—
y acerca, aleja,
me, le, nos
da
cabida.

3. MERRY-GO-ROUND

Three horses came down the hill
and sumptuously entered
the river's transparency.
One
waded out next to me.
At times, it paused to drink.
At times, it looked me in the eye.
And between us both,
an ancient murmur passed
on its sojourn.

Your three horses, stallions, studs.
With their hooves plunged into the mud
and water at their haunches
laving their bellies.
Drinking and grazing
on the undulation of their silhouettes.
One, that one there,
the sorrel
whose sadness reminds me of a childhood mare
my father swapped
for two dappled grays,
caught me by surprise, dreaming:
in the moistness of our eyes,
manes riffling, weeds trailing in water,
a private space orients
—me, it, us—
in nearness, then lets
me, it, us
fall
away.

Eco

in memoriam Emily Dickinson

. . . no sonaría tan hondo
de ser producto del firmamento,
aires de océano sin fondo . . .

A flote entre tu cristalino
y tu mirada,
lo último que pasa
por mi materia gris
y su salutífera
delicuescencia
es
si sabré o no nadar,
si podré respirar,
si viviré como antes.

Me contiene la ampolla
de tu aliento.
Me encierra con llave.
Me trastorna.

Confinada a hablar sola,
digo y escucho,
pregunto y *me* respondo.
Tarareo, creo cantar,
inhalo, inhalo y no reviento.
Soy nadie.

Tras la tapia
de hidrógeno y oxígeno,
clarísima, diríase iluminada,
me permites concebir
que *el agua es la raíz del viento*
y huele a sales, a microbios,
a intimidad la atmósfera.

Echo

In memoriam Emily Dickinson

It would not sound so deep
Were it a Firmamental Product—
Airs no Oceans keep—

Afloat between your lens
and your gaze,
the last consideration to go
across my gray matter
and its salubrious
deliquescence
is
whether or not I'll swim,
whether I'll be able to breathe,
whether I'll live as before.

I'm caught in the bubble
of your breath.
It locks me in.
Drives me mad.

Confined to speak alone,
I talk and listen,
question and answer *myself*.
I hum, I think I sing,
I breathe in, breathe in and don't explode.
I'm no one.

Behind the wall
of hydrogen and oxygen,
very clear, almost illuminated,
you allow me to think
that *the Root of the Wind is Water*
and the atmosphere
smells of salt and microbes and intimacy.

Y en el acto viene
el *eco*
de un más allá de más allá,
lengua arcaica y empapada
de sílabas y acentos aptos
para re-de-trans formar,
dar luz,
dar a luz a
melanina
oculta en otra piel:
hueco de la voz,
la que habla sola.

And in that instant comes
the *low echo*
of a *beyond* beyond,
a language archaic and soaked
in syllables and accents suited
for re-de-trans-forming,
bringing light
which brings out
melanin
from beneath another skin:
the *hollow* of a voice
which speaks alone.

Llaga profunda

I.
Sólo la cercanía,
selvática
y a la vez vacía,
pone al ras
la avidez de sol
de las heridas,
las llagas vivas
que al supurar consuelan
por lo puro,
la fetidez de su fuerza
blanca.
Como un cítrico
sin jugos
cuya pulpa
ya se está pudriendo.

Deep Wound

I.
Only proximity,
trees in a forest
with emptiness between them,
rouses us to recognize
that our wounds hunger
for sunlight,
these living lesions that
as they suppurate
console us with their purity,
the fetidness of their white
force.
Like a mottled
orange,
its pulp
already rotten.

2.

No todas las niñas, las muchachas en flor,
adornan las riberas de las frescas corrientes
que perfilan los valles de la infancia.
Algunas sienten sobre sí
al cisne que avasalló a Leda,
insulsas, insensatas, incapaces
de saborear el blancor intenso de sus plumas,
la elegancia curva de su cuello,
su salmodiar en éxtasis.
Qué tal que se tratara de un arcángel
en lugar de un animal.
Qué tal que le insuflara
el silabario
del placer y del dolor.

2.

Not all the girls, budding young women,
spackle the banks of the nervous rivers
that churn through childhood's valleys.
Some of them sense, bearing down,
the swan that mastered Leda;
vapid, insensate, they can't
relish the white splendor of its feathers,
the gracile elegance of its neck,
its ecstatic hymn.
But if it were an archangel
instead of an animal?
And if he could breath into her
the syllabary
of pleasure and pain?

3.

Cumbre ascendida
en pos de escenas sin pasado,
descifrada sin querer.

Queja arrancada de raíz,
bulbo
áspero y sin sino.

3.

Searching for scenes without a past,
I came to the climax
and deciphered it unintentionally.

A moan yanked up by the root,
a bitter bulb
devoid of destiny.

Almendra

Tuve primero su conjunto melódico
dentro de la pituitaria:
su soltura melancólica en descenso
a los oídos
y la cueva, la gruta armónica
de pespunte y contrapunto:
tres consonantes enlazadas,
su emisión unísona.
Su nutriente
engaño
se cifraba
en mi entrada
a la enorme estancia
iluminada
para robar el fuego,
un puñado de semillas,
centros del mundo ahusados.

Habiendo recorrido en arco
la velocidad de ese minuto
—este mismo
a la hora de la hora
al ahora del ahora
ala hora—,
escucho al masticar:
qué latidos,
qué susurros
compactos
y ambrosinos.

Consonantes trituradas
sin gastar saliva en balde
se repiten, se digieren,
se repiten sin cesar
ene dé erre ene dé erre
n d r   n d r

Almond

I first heard its melodic chorus
in my pituitary:
its fluent melancholy channeling
down through my ears
into a harmonic grotto,
backstitch and counterpoint:
a vowel and two interlaced consonants
making their unified report.
Its nourishing
allure
became coded
to my entrance
into that big, brightly
lit room
of pilfered fire,
my fistful of seeds,
the centers of a spindled world.

Going over the speed
of the span of that minute
—this same one
the hour of the hour
the now of the now
owl hour—
I can hear chewing:
an incredible throbbing,
and dense
ambrosial
whispers.

A vowel and two consonants
worth the spit it takes
to chew them, repeat, and digest
them one after another
ah el em   ah el em
alm   alm

mientras el líquido
en fuga
penetra
en amargor de sangre
en sabor de golpe
de un producto
de la tierra
de husos filosos,
signos que interrogan
y se admiran
desde otras geografías, desiertos,
dátiles, oasis, moléculas en árabe
y ahora penetran a las mías,
por la punta de la lengua.

as the trickling
liquid
passes into
my blood's bitterness
with its rush of taste,
the loamy
gleaning
of cracked bones,
of queries
and surprises
from distant geographies, deserts,
dates, oases, Arabic molecules
pervading my own
through the tip of my tongue.

Acaso Borneo

. . . debo ser tu guía y quien te lleve
desde este sitio humilde hasta otro eterno . . .
—DANTE, *El Infierno*, Canto I

Desde la madreperla de cualquier nombre
que va escorando, apuntalando
a uno entre muchos semejantes,
se abre un túnel
insondable,
y el atisbo
de su equivalente equidistante.
No su igual.

Digo
anturio o alstromelia
y se enciende alguna flor
de un infernal color de rosa
y otra de pétalos rayados
sobre fondo sin fin;
floresta,
y emerge
el Siglo de Oro,
su modo de bautizar
un bosque ameno.
Algo me secretea:
si cantaras en letanía
el entrevero de aquel huerto infantil,
caimito, nance, zaramullo, chinalima,
resonarían selvas interiores.

꩜

En nada de esto pensabas tú
en compañía del príncipe indonesio.

Maybe Borneo

. . . follow me and I will be your guide
and lead you from here through an eternal place . . .
—DANTE, *The Inferno*, Canto I

From the nacre of any name
that starts a list to specify
one among others of a kind,
an unfathomable
tunnel opens
and a glimpse
of some equidistant equivalence.
—Not congruence.

I say
anthurium or narcissus
and so light up some ridiculously
pink-colored flower
or one with petals fringing
an endless depth;
a thicket,
and out of it comes
The Golden Age
when a forest could be
baptized *beneficent.*
Something says to me in secret:
if you would chant a litany
to that chaotic orchard of your childhood,
the *caimito, nance, zaramullo,* and *chinalima* trees,
it would all arboresce inside you.

None of this crossed your mind
when you fell together with the Indonesian prince.

Lo innombrable
te mantuvo

a distancia, en reverencia.

Iba en busca de su niña,
natural de esos paisajes
como él mismo o su prosapia,
tanto así
que no podía extraviarse nunca
entre, cabe, sobre, cerca, a orillas de
aquellos manantiales, remolinos
como la palma de su mano.

Su vida,
filial apego a cierta geografía,
te mantuvo
lejos. No demasiado.
No para impedir que a ti llegara
el aullido bestial
del instrumento de aliento
de un corazón
que lo ha perdido todo.

Sollozaba el hombre
el monarca
el padre
ante un cadáver infantil
en la ribera.
La maleza, la maleza, la maleza
no lograba ensordecer la pena:

los nombres escondidos
en el milenario juncal
comenzaron a danzar
al ritmo de las lluvias

The unnamable
held you

at a distance, in reverence.

He went looking for his daughter
who was, like himself or his ancestors,
a native of those landscapes
and knew them so well
she could never get lost
within, along, above, near, beside
those springs and whirlpools
familiar as the palm of her hand.

His life,
his filial bond to that territory,
held you
at a distance. But not too far.
Not so far that
you couldn't hear
within the wind
the bestial bellow
of a soul
that had lost everything.

The man
the monarch
the father sobbed
before a child's corpse
on the riverbank.
And none of that undergrowth, undergrowth, undergrowth
could muffle his grief:

the names concealed
by sullen weeds
began to twirl
to the beat of a torrential,

torrenciales, cadenciosas,
vueltos plegaria volátil,
cuerpo inconsútil,
endecha
que se eleva al polo norte
o a la Antártica en invierno,
rezumando entre las miles de maneras
de distinguir, en este mundo,
un color blanco de otro:
un color nieve tierna,
uno para el frío acumulado varios meses
—albo superlativo—,
un color hielo a punto,
todo tan sí mismo como caluroso el verde
al otro lado, al sur de las fronteras,
el verde intenso, verde sólo planta o malaquita,
musgo en la piedra, en el acantilado,
breña o tupido matorral,
qué más da,
y el que denota, connota, anota
un palidecer, un carecer, un prescindir
de tintes y matices poco a poco
hasta la saciedad de la nada
para ser más adelante
llamarada amarilla o color naranja,
fuego frutal
neozelandés
o de un Borneo no imaginario
de latitud malaya
alcanzable
con un grito. Un desgarramiento real.

Aguas unas y otras.
De caudaloso y nemoroso afluente
o de témpano diluido.
La misma historia.

cadenced rain,
lifting into the air as prayers,
as a seamless body,
a dirge
rising toward the north pole
or to wintry Antarctica,
seeping into the thousands of ways
to designate, in the here and now,
one color of white against another:
the color of virgin snow
and the color of snow frozen for months
—a superlative albescence—
the precise color of ice,
everything as much itself as the sweltering green
on the far side, the southern frontier,
that intense green, green of plants or malachite,
moss on stones, on the cliff,
brambles or heavy thickets,
what difference does it make,
and the color that denotes, connotes, notes
a fading away, a falling off, an endless
diminishment of shades and hues
little by little satiating the nothingness
so later it might
flare up yellow or orange,
fiery as fruit
from New Zealand
or from some unimagined Borneo
in the Malayan latitudes
just a shout
away. A vivid tearing apart.

Water of every kind.
From rushing, sylvan streams
to melting icebergs.
The same story.

Las mismas lágrimas
de alegría,
de congoja,
de afán
de escurrirse uno entero
por la piel, desde los poros y hasta el suelo,
quedar seco y luego
prolongarse entre la tierra,
reconocer su *sangre de mi sangre*
hasta la locura
o su equivalente equidistante.

De verbo en verbo
de selva en selva
de polo en polo
de tú a tú . . .
En lengua *ngaju*,
se entiende,
o por sabido
se calla.

Un dolor borroso, indefinido
te mantuvo
en vilo
en este globo
con un pie en cada hemisferio.
Tan absurdo cual humano.
Tan humano cual divino.
Tan humilde como eterno.

The same tears
of rapture,
grief,
anxiety,
of being wrung out completely,
from top to bottom,
and left desiccated and then
persevering in the dirt,
recognizing *the blood of my blood*
right up into madness
or its equidistant equivalence.

From verb to verb
from forest to forest
from pole to pole
from thou to thou . . .
In the Ngaju tongue,
it's understood,
or being known,
goes without saying.

A vague, indefinite pain
held you
suspended
on this globe
one foot in each hemisphere.
As absurd as it is human.
As human as it is divine.
As humbling as it is eternal.

II

Dos poemas luctuosos,
tardíos

II

Two Poems of Mourning
(Belatedly)

El cuadro de mi vida

I. MUJER SOBRE FONDO VERDE
Cómo habrá llegado a mí
tu rostro,
entre aromas, fragancias (tú escoge)
de las flores de seda de un sombrero anticuado
y las flores de camposanto
en el dorso de unas manos
sin contornos:
el retrato sólo llega hasta los hombros . . .

Quizás todo afloró
como se había esfumado,
flotando por los aires
de alguna indefensión,
un pavor alado,
una imagen trunca, recuperada
y nacida para animar qué cosa,
una cierta familiaridad
que, vista de cerca,
asustaría por ajena.

Aún cual fantasmagoría
carente del impacto cara a cara,
tus pupilas me absorbieron
y llevaron de paseo
por la secuencia en blanco y negro
de alguien muerto de todo morir:
nacimiento, kimono, diversos uniformes,
Te Deum, traje de novia,
luna de miel en el puerto,
múltiples alumbramientos;
peinada, sin peinar, despeinada;
cabello restirado, en alto, con crepé;
recién teñido, sin teñir;

My Life's Portrait

I. WOMAN AGAINST A GREEN BACKGROUND
How will it appear to me,
your face,
cloaked in aromas, fragrances (you choose)
of silk flowers on an old-fashioned hat
and with age spots
on the back of your shapeless
hands:
the portrait comes only to your shoulders.

Maybe everything blossomed
like it was going up in smoke,
floated on the airs
of some vulnerability,
a winged terror,
a truncated image, rescued
and given life just to animate what?
—a familiarity
that, seen up close,
would be scarily alien.

Even as a phantasmagoria
too insubstantial for face-to-face impact,
your pupils absorbed me
and carried me off
through the black-and-white sequences
of the truly dead dead:
swaddling, kimono, various uniforms,
Te Deum, bridesgown,
honeymoon at the beach,
a number of childbirths;
hair coiffed, uncombed, completely tangled;
slicked back, piled up, teased out;
recently dyed, natural;

y tras la puerta,
el idilio de alguien consigo
reflejando
el revés al derecho:
caballete, paleta, tubos de pintura,
aguarrás, aguarrás, aguarrás,
tan raro y embriagante
como los paisajes que irías
diluyendo con tu plasma:
los jardines borrosos de la melancolía,
la pileta de mosaico de tu júbilo inconfeso,
figuras en las nubes,
montañas, montes, colinas, cerros, valles,
altiplanos del para qué o quién sentimental,
frascos que contendrían el fruncido ceño,
león feroz, encerrado en este mundo:
todo una evocación apenas,
una franja en nuestro firmamento.

and behind the door,
your own illusion
reflecting back
in reverse:
painting stand, palette, tubes of paint,
turpentine, turpentine, turpentine,
so strange and inebriating
like those landscapes you would wash out
with your own plasma:
the smudged, melancholy gardens,
the mosaic basin of your unconfessed exultation,
shapes in the clouds,
mountains, alps, hills, foothills, valleys,
the high plains of the sentimental whom or whatever,
bottles that reflected your scowl,
ferocious as a lion, buried in the world,
and all this scarcely an evocation,
a mere fringe in the firmament.

2. GUSARAPO SOBRE FONDO AZUL

Clara persona
de ocho años,
en tránsito de lo posible
a lo vergonzoso.

Reinventada
en actitud de niña buena,
que aprende a no ser ella,
a estarse quieta, casi inmóvil,
a posar
de ahí para el real.
La expresión en el rostro, fabulosa.

Un vestido de terciopelo púrpura
con cuello de tira bordada;
calcetines perfectamente doblados
a la altura del tobillo,
zapatos nuevos de charol.
Pero las manos nuevamente
se le escapan al artista . . .

De largo pasan.
Y a posar obligan
a todo lo demás.
Posar mirando aquel jardín
y su interminable torbellino
hasta el colmo del mareo,
hasta desplomarse en el pasto
y comprobar
que al no girar el cuerpo,
comenzaban a dar vueltas las estrellas;
el telescopio en los ojos
se volvía entonces un embudo
que absorbía delirio a cuentagotas . . .
Al rehusarme a ser
naturaleza muerta,
perdí el único asidero.

2. WATERWORM AGAINST A BLUE BACKGROUND

A radiant
eight year old
on her way from the possible
to the shameful.

Reinvented
in the guise of a good girl
who learns to not be herself,
to sit still, all but immobile,
to adopt a pose
from this moment on.
The expression on her face, fabulous.

A dress of purple velvet
with a lacy collar;
socks conscientiously folded down
to the top of the ankle,
new patent leather shoes.
But her hands once again
escape the artist . . .

They reach into the future.
And they oblige
everything else to pose.
As she would pose and stare at that garden
with its interminable whirlwind
and the dizziness would intensify
until she tumbled into the grass
and discovered
that when her body wasn't spinning around,
the stars themselves were circling;
then the telescopes in her eyes
would gradually funnel
away the delirium bit by bit . . .
Because I refused to be
a still life,
I lost the only grip I had.

El mismo cordón que me soltó
se me enredó en el cuello,
transparente nudo
corredizo en la garganta,
mientras se presentían
luciérnagas
tras los barrotes
de unos puños
tácitos.

The very cord that set me free
was twisted around my neck,
a transparent slipknot
choking me
while fireflies
flickered
between the bars of my fingers
as I made
a fist.

3. NIÑA SOBRE FONDO OSCURO

Desde mi anagnórisis augusta,
mi percatarme
de esa parte abolida e insignificante
pero absuelta,
que se arrojará a los cuatro vientos
diseminándose entre pajas, puntas de alas, uñas,
lágrimas, anhelos, naderías
que aún llevan la voz cantante,
exigí la devolución material de la inmateria,
una persona pintada por sí misma,
pintada de nacimiento,
pintada per se.
Alguien leyó abismo en todo esto:
"No estás tú para saberlo,
pero el botín ya estaba repartido".

 ✐

Un organismo respira
dentro de una bolsa
de plástico negra,
una bolsa de basura.
Se está asfixiando.
Pero así quiere seguir.
No me atrevo
a quitarle la vida
haciéndolo cruzar
el umbral oxigenado.
Qué pasaría al hallarnos frente a frente.
Qué, quién
se salvaría . . .

[Háblame, plástico negro
tu lenguaje sí lo entiendo,
a ti qué más te da
enviar cadáveres de guerra,
lucir el color triste, insoportable

3. GIRL AGAINST A DARK BACKGROUND
From self-awareness,
a grave perception
of some speck of me—abolished and inconsequential
but absolved,
lost to the four winds
dehiscent with bits of straw, wingtips, fingernails,
tears, longing, the ratty nothings
that direct everything else,
I insisted I wanted back that material from the immaterial,
that painting of the woman who painted herself,
who was born painted,
who painted *per se.*
Someone read abyss in all of this:
"You may not recall, but
you mother's booty was already parceled out."

An organism is panting
inside a black
plastic bag,
a trash bag.
Almost asphyxiated,
but persevering.
I don't dare
snip its life
by pulling it out
across the threshold of air.
What would happen were we to come face to face.
What, who
would be saved . . .

[Talk to me, black plastic,
yes, I think I understand your language,
and you, you don't care whether you're
stuffed with corpses from the war,
you flaunt the same sad, unbearable

de mi falda aquella vez,
del filo de la esquela, el crespón,
el listón de luto en cuello blanco almidonado,
el deseo
de morir
en serio.]

Hasta entonces,
la bolsa
se inflaba
y desinflaba
a ritmo fijo,
cardiaco.
[Nadie más se daba cuenta.]
Cada vez más fuerte,
duplicado,
de fosas nasales,
de pulmones,
de ventrículos
que coinciden
con tus pozos.

Aparécete tal cual,
resonó
la luz
desde mi puño abierto:

Te vi al fin.
Me vi por fin.
A nadie pude recordar.

color of the dress I once wore,
with its death-letter black border, its crepe
mourning ribbon hung from a starched collar,
and a sincere
desire
to die.]

Until then,
the bag
inflates
and deflates
with a fixed rhythm,
cardiacal.
[No one else sees it.]
Each time stronger,
a kind of doubling,
as nostrils are doubled
and lungs,
and ventricles
that coincide
with the wells of your eyes.

Show yourself!
the light
bears down
on my opening fist:

Finally I saw you.
I saw myself finally.
There was no one to tell.

Diálogo de las cenizas

Somos *casi* pura agua
que acaso se integre
al amoroso ardor
del agua pura

No como Cicerón
en *su* sabia admonición
a Catilina,
o como algún sacerdote poeta
predicando desde *su* púlpito,
sino como un muerto
que enterrará a *sus* muertos,
me disuelvo
en platónico intercambio
entre lo que atrás quedó
y lo que hoy se desmorona,
un mero rezago vital,
una zanja que se ahonda
conforme pierde nitidez.

Va uno abandonando el mundo
—todavía en el cuerpo—
ante quien llena formularios,
autoriza,
da el sí
a una permuta
en cenicienta bagatela.

De los relatos infantiles tan diversos,
siempre preferí el de aquella niña,
lánguida, bella, abandonada,
siempre vestida igual, delantal, chal,
sobre sus hombros el mal,
ella, a quien le echaron la sal,
protegida sólo

Dialogue of the Ashes

We're *almost* pure water
composed, perhaps, of
the amorous ardor
of poured water

Not like Cicero
in *his* thoughtful admonition
to Catalina,
or like some poet-priest
expounding from *his* pulpit,
but more like one of the dead
who bury *their* own dead,
I dissolve
in a Platonic interchange
between what I left behind
and what is reduced to crumbs,
a modest, vital withholding,
a crevasse that gets murkier
the deeper you look into it.

While someone abandons the world
—although the body remains—
someone else fills out forms,
marking yes,
permitting
the Cinderella-like transformation
into a knickknack of ashes.

From all those childhood stories,
I preferred the one about that girl,
languid, lovely, abandoned,
forever in the same clothes, apron, shawl,
her misfortune weighing on her shoulders,
she, at whom they hissed and threw salt,
protected only

por una emoción
desde ultratumba.

Yo soy la nueva cenicienta sin tizne
y como de zetas se trata
atenazada, jugando con fuego,
entre dos urnas
que apenas pesan,
abrasada, abrazada,
estirada hasta que truenen y revienten
las articulaciones entre la santa cruz
y el ángel atado
a un edificio de concreto
(cual mariposa negra, shmahaná,
ave de mal agüero
o murciélago de vocales cantarinas
pero igualmente lúgubre apariencia
clavado con daga a un lienzo,
al lado de otras alas coloridas,
sujetas con livianísimo alfiler),
sobre un fondo sólido,
un cielo plomizo
citadino.

Abrir las dos moradas
y contradecir
su "perpetuidad".
Dejar que las dos urnas
pierdan la tapa,
volarles la tapa
aunque yo pierda
el piso y la cabeza.
Y qué.
Dos orificios en este gran esquema,
en este gran planeta,
letras que aspiran a mayúsculas
e inspiran una subyacente calidad

by an emotion
from beyond.

Here I come, the new Cinderella, minus the cinders,
and while all those S sounds hang in the air, let me say
I've been seared stirring up a fire
between two urns
that weigh almost nothing,
scorched, pricked,
stretched to the point of snapping, of blowing out
ligaments between the chancel cross
and an angel pinned
to the concrete wall
(like a black butterfly,
a bird of ill-omen,
or a vowel-chirping bat, Chiroptera,
no less lugubrious
spiked with a knife to a canvas
next to other colored wings
held in place with thin pins),
over a solid background,
a leaden, urban
sky.

To open the two resting places
and interrupt
their "perpetuity."
To allow the tops
of both urns to be pried off,
to fly off,
although I lose
my own mind and bearings.
But so what.
Two holes in this weighty scheme,
on this splendid planet,
letters that aspire to capitalization
and inspire an underlying quality,

subalterna
subordinada
subtodo
y más que nada
sublime
[oh, voz,
tú sí gravitas significando
a cada paso más y más,
buscándote en torno
y hallándote al centro
de un inmenso catafalco,
tú, momia sin vendajes,
momia expuesta tan visible y descarnada].

Y el finísimo polvo
hará de tripas corazón
y de corazón lábil tolvanera
para que dos bocas extintas
reposen dialogando.
Cenizas de hueso calcinado, unas,
y de hueso cernido por los años,
otras . . .
¿Qué hacer con semejante mezcla
de actos fallidos y afortunados?
¿Con qué derecho
dispondrá esta atmósfera
de polvos de vísperas, polvos de víctimas,
polvos vírgenes de dos pobres feligreses
que creyeron conducirse según mandato
incomprensible e insoslayable
inalcanzable e infinito
inmarcesible e incontenible
cuanto indeclinable,
el único y verdadero mandato,
básica, profunda, sola,
solemnemente lingüístico?
¿En qué página de qué diccionario

one that's subaltern,
subordinate,
subducted,
and more than anything
sublime
[oh, voice,
yes, you are sinking nearer, signifying
more and more each time,
searching only to find
yourself at the center of a kind
of immense catafalque, you,
a mummy unwrapped,
a mummy so vividly defleshed and exposed.]

And the finest dust
of intention
will whirl up from the labile heart
so that those two extinguished mouths
might once again talk.
Dust of parched ribs, fingernails,
and bones sifted by the years,
by others . . .
What to make of this mix
of failed and triumphal acts?
What right does
the atmosphere have
to disperse this vesperal dust, this victim dust,
this virgin dust of two poor believers
who came to act according to a mandate
incomprehensible and insoluble
unreachable and infinite
undying and uncontainable
as well as undeniable,
a simple and true mandate,
basically, profoundly, singularly,
and solemnly linguistic?
On what page of the dictionary

se esconde la definición de este misterio,
en qué párrafo de qué divina narración,
en qué ficción que aterre
desgañitándose:
hay una gran oscuridad
en el claror de la belleza,
hay oscuridad que encierra,
que bajo el seudónimo de soledad
ha forjado y se ha tragado la llave?
¿En qué canto de pájaro de la antigua Alhambra,
en tonos arábigos, hebraicos y latinos,
de selvas rumorosas
o de grabados a punta seca de altos vuelos
se esconderá el eco de quienes
bordaron su mortaja
a tiempo
a cambio
de una eternidad
plena
de sílabas, diptongos, hiatos?

Me he colgado de sus voces
para sobrevivir de este lado del enigma.
Porque es lo único que logro retener:
notas que día con día van conformando
algo profundo y suave, paternal,
melodioso, imaginable, maternal,
en lo que cifro
por escrito,
en tan efímero
e infantil
réquiem.

do we find this mystery's revelation,
in what paragraph of what divine narration,
in what terrifying fiction
lost in its own telling:
or is fiction only a vast darkness
inside the clarity of beauty,
a darkness that closes in,
that, under the pseudonym of solitude,
has forged and swallowed the key?
In what birdsong from the old Alhambra,
in Arabic, Hebrew, and Latin accents,
from whispering forests
or from fine dry-point prints
can we find the echo of those who
stitched their shrouds
in time
to exchange them for
an eternity
filled
with syllables, diphthongs, hiatus?

I've clung to those voices
just to survive on this side of the enigma.
Because it's the only thing I've been able to keep:
notes that day by day gather into
something profound and gentle, paternal,
melodious, imagined, maternal,
in all I cipher
through writing,
in this ephemeral
and infantile
requiem.

Fábula disuelta, ensimismada

A Mil y Canga,
por nuestro ningún lado

Poder decir

sin puntuación

momento júbilo infinito
júbilo infinito momento
infinito momento júbilo
algarabía
y por si fuera poco
arde y canta
solipsista
sin que nadie
más que la propia
extraña entraña
ajena al mundo
la comparta

Poder decir

sin artilugios,
filigranas,
subrayados o cursivas

supremo instante
de gozo
sin orillas
al centro de una inmensidad
sin apremio de auxilio alguno
a sabiendas de que las fuerzas
escapan ligeras del músculo
y se van volando
y uno hundiendo

Dehiscent, Enraptured Invention

To Mil and Canga
for our nowhere land

To be able to speak

without punctuation

jubilant infinite moment
moment jubilant infinite
infinite moment jubilant
gibberish
and as if that weren't enough
to burn and sing
a solipsist
heard
by no one
beyond
the weird world's
distant core

To be able to speak

without contrivance,
filigrees,
underlinings or cursives

supreme instant
of unbounded
pleasure
at the center of an immensity
without any outside pressure
knowing that the vital forces
peel away from muscle easily
and drift off
and you drown

y no importa
pues se está a buen resguardo
ensimismado

Poder decir

decirlo
decírselo
uno
a uno
de consuno

Poder decir

una tarde esplendorosa
recién lavadas estiradas tendidas
las nubes
entre azul
y buenas noches
avanzando a buen paso
por un camino recorrido
innumerables veces
como si fuera la primera
o la única
como una y única esta bóveda
como esta tierra andada en redondez
completa
vamos cantando
la misma canción de siempre
cantada innumerables veces
como si fuera la primera
la única

Poder decir

una tarde de una vida
en que ustedes

and it doesn't matter
since you're protected
enraptured

To be able to speak

to speak it
to speak it to you
one
to oneself
consubstantial

To be able to speak

splendid the afternoon
clouds
freshly rinsed stirred tended
between blue
and goodnight
coming to a decent end
along a road taken
innumerable times
as if it were the first
or the only
as this firmament is single and singular
as this earth has been traversed
all the way around
on we go singing
the same song always
over and over
as if it were the first
the only

To be able to speak

an afternoon of a life
in which

absortos en la música
se ingieren
se devoran
se beben a sorbitos
porque cada nota
es un espejo
maravillosamente único
sagradamente
cóncavo y convexo
y por fortuna
imperceptible

Poder decir

una vida en una tarde
en que conduzco
este mi funicular
desde la casualidad
hasta el destino
me deja alcanzarlos
e ingerirlos
embebidos en sí mismos
cantando los tres
los tres cantando

Poder decir

a un lado dan sus tonos
orquestados afinados
oyameles encinos
en fortísimo contraste
con la coloratura purpurina
de jacarandas jacarandas jacarandas

y al otro
entre teatrales y líricos
tabachines llamaradas bugambilias

absorbed in the music
you all are swallowed
devoured
gulped down
because each note
is a mirror
marvelously singular
sacredly
concave and convex
and fortunately
imperceptible

To be able to speak

an afternoon of a life,
in which I drive
this my funicular
from chance
to destiny
where I meet you
and drink you in
who are drunk on yourselves
singing all three of us
the three of us singing

To be able to speak

the tones on one side
orchestrated arranged
by pine-trees oaks
in a *fortissimo* contrasting
with the glittering coloratura
of jacarandas jacarandas jacarandas

and on the other side
among theaters and lyrics
poincianas trumpet-vines bougainvilleas

flor de mayo anticipada o retrasada
y a través del parabrisas
el cristal trasero y los espejos laterales
las copas amplias
alvéolos esponjados
entretelas de nuestro personal espacio abstracto
en robles cedros y más que aromáticos abetos

desde las profundidades
del alinde
emerge
la nota baja
entrecortada
finamente
por una voz quebrada
plumas multicolores que desde ella ascienden
en aras y alas de una lírica
que me define
a las afueras
de pies a cabeza
genio y figura
del maternal sonido

poder decir

por decir algo

poder decir

early or late mayflowers
and through the windshield
the rear glass
and the side windows
the spongy alveoli
of full treetops
the folds of our personally abstract space
rendered as oaks cedars and more-than-aromatic firs

from the depths
of the reflecting glass
emerges
the low note
finely
parsed
by a broken voice
from which colored feathers rise
in the rush of a lyricism
which defines me
to a T,
head to foot
spirit and form
of sound

to be able to speak

by speaking, so to speak

to speak

Y el anturio, impávido

Dos abejorros
le extraen el jugo,
dulce y amargo,
al centro
de las hojas color de rosa
de una flor que no es rosa.
Ahítos,
golpean los ventanales
vez tras vez,
seguros de emigrar,
con el tesoro adentro,
allende el aire,
ignorantes del eclipse
de un sendero libre,
ignorantes
del imán
de un espejismo.
Con la sangre miel
en las entrañas,
parte ya de una médula
extática.
Y distinta.

And the Intrepid Anthurium

Two bumblebees
extract nectar,
sweet and bitter
from the center
of the rose-colored petals
of a flower which is not a rose.
Sated,
they thud against the picture window
again and again,
fixed on escaping
with their bounty inside them,
into the air behind them,
incognizant that the path to freedom
has been eclipsed,
incognizant
that they are drawn
to an illusion.
With the blood honey
in their guts
already a part of their
rapturous marrow.
And distinct.

Qué escándalo

PRIMER COMPÁS
Irreproducibles acordes
idénticos a tu antes
y a tu más allá.
Tu ahora.
Ronquido pausado,
constante,
con que acompañas tus clavados
desde una plataforma altísima
—un arco construido a lo lejos—
a una piscina
de agua limpia,
solos tú y tu alma
emergiendo luego
a un universo
de cacofonías diamantinas.

ÚLTIMO COMPÁS
Silbido.
La inconfundible vuelta a casa,
el despertar de un trance hipnótico.
Pulcritud del tubo central
del órgano de una antigua catedral,
la sala de conciertos
de tu vida:

un acento principesco,
fin y principio;
un mucho gusto aliterado
y mi correspondiente
no te olvido alicaído.
Silbido en fuga
colibríes en persecución,
testigos de un descanso en paz,
un desplomarse

The Roar

The identical
chords of your before
and your afterwards.
Your now.
The slow, steady
snore
you bring with you into those high
platform dives into sleep
—an arc devised at a remove—
into a pool
of clear water,
you alone and your soul
emerging later
into a universe
of diamantine cacophony.

LAST TEMPO
Hiss.
The incomparable return home,
as though waking from a hypnotic trance.
The consummate beauty of that central pipe
in the organ of an ancient cathedral,
the concert hall
of your life:

a princely accent,
first and last;
your assonant *thank you too*
and my corresponding
I won't forget you barely audible.
A fugitive hiss,
tortured hummingbirds,
witnesses to a breach in the peace,
tumbling

de una rama a otra
y nunca más ascender
e implosionarse.
Todo chisporroteo molecular,
brevísimo hallazgo.

Rasguño de la pluma fuente sobre la hoja de papel,
de la pluma verde esmeralda sobre la hoja de árbol,
mano y ave implumes
por la rapidez del movimiento.

CODA
Dime cómo
apaciguarme antes
del descenso y el descanso,
acompasadamente
rescatada
y al rescate
del escándalo
en silencio.

from one branch to another,
never again to rise
flapping.
All those molecular sparks
but only the briefest revelation.

The scratch of the pen's tip against a leaf of paper,
of the green tree tip against a leaf,
hand and bird deplumed
by the sheer speed of things.

CODA
Tell me how
to calm myself before
the descent and what follows,
how to be rhythmically
resuscitated
so I might resuscitate
that roar
in the silence.

Cor cordis

En la pobre, débil carne
proliferada y suplicante
no hay memoria del dolor.
No hay
imagen fidedigna
sazonada al máximo
detalle anatómico
que lo recuerde.
Registro en la idea,
pero no vuelto a sentir.
Mirada atrás en el hoy
que se prepara
y no quisiera en el después
lo que se alojó
dentro
antes.

El alivio mata
el espasmo
de los nervios
atrapados,
elimina,
borra
todo,
hasta el tronar de huesos,
el desgarrar de músculo y tendón,
el rompe y rasga de membranas
que dan vida.
O el increíble
paso sin marcar
que lejos de facilitar avance
propicia el paro
en el sagrado templo
de lo, el, la innombrable.

Heart's Core

In our poor, weak flesh,
multiplied and supplicant,
the memory of pain fades.
There's
no reliable image
rendered to the last
anatomical detail
that can be remembered.
I register the thought
but don't come again to the feeling.
Glancing back on the day
that readies itself,
I wouldn't want, in what comes next,
anything that abided
in
before.

Relief snuffs
the spasm
of trapped
nerves,
eliminates,
erases
everything
until the bones pop,
muscles tear from tendon,
and life-giving membranes
rend and rupture.
Oh the fabulous
pacemaker,
instead of stoking the beat,
it stimulates the stroke
in the sacred temple
of this, thine, the unnameable.

Del paso al paro
o viceversa.
Ni un niño,
armado de impoluta fantasía,
es capaz de revivir
lo mutilado,
el ardor de alguna bofetada.

Pero
una frase
cortada a la medida,
filoso y negro dardo de ónix,
vuelve a chisporrotear en las entrañas,
con toda su carga atómica,
siniestra.
Curioso que en ella no burbujeen sino latidos.
Que entre palabras
viva el cor cordis,
no el registro.
Ahí sí que no hay olvido del dolor.
Ahí sí que resplandece,
candente,
su memoria:
su impacto se renueva
sin tener que articularla
a voz en cuello.
Y después, sólo la condición
de los heridos en combate,
los caídos;
y ni sombra de aquel talón
de Aquiles
posado con cuidado,
ni sus luces.
Deleznabilidad
de la mente incauta,
prensada invisiblemente

From stoke to stroke
or vice versa.
Not even a child,
armed with purest fantasy
could revive
what is ravaged,
the ardor of such a blow.

But
a certain sentence
perfectly measured,
a sharp, black onyx dart,
keeps hitting the target inside me
with all its sinister, atomic
plunk.
How curious that it feels less like prickling than throbbing.
That between words
we find the *heart's core*,
not merely an account of it.
There, where pain isn't forgotten.
There, where memory
radiates,
candescent:
its signal strength enduring
with no need
to plead its case.
And next comes the condition
shared by those wounded in combat,
the stricken:
not the shadow of some
Achilles heel
poised so carefully
and then withdrawn into thin air.
The fragility
of an imprudent mind
carried invisibly

por armas de dos filos,
lenguas afiladas,
oraciones
en pos de alturas
expresivas.

by two-edged arms,
razor-edged tongues,
prayers
aimed at *expressive*
heights.

Pasa

. . . nos baña de locura, enloquece a la montaña,
requiebra a la mujer, sana al lunático,
incorpora a los muertos, pide el Viático . . .
—RAMÓN LÓPEZ VELARDE

       por el minúsculo orificio
       de la aherrojada cerradura
       de la reja del patio
       que da al jardín
       y a la azotehuela
       de mis ojos
       sin importar nada
       más que la llave
       y el chirrido
       que deja sueltos
       sala, comedor,
       cocina,
       recámara,
       cuna, roperos,
       imágenes de santos,
       cama con cabecera,
       alguien ahí,
       tú,
       lentamente incorporándote,
       un espacio vacío a tu lado
       y, en el aire,
       el no se diga más
       o esta boca es mía.
       Y el trueno, la tormenta,
       los rayos y centellas,
       las descargas todas,
       un mero
       telón de fondo
       que rime con hondo.

Come On In

. . . bathes us in madness, maddens the mountain,
flirts with the woman, cures the crazy,
raises the dead, demands the Viaticum . . .
—RAMÓN LÓPEZ VELARDE

through a tiny hole
in the rusted lock
of the patio gate
that opens to the garden
and to the rooftop
of my eyes
signifying nothing
more than the key itself
and its click
which discloses a view of
living room, dining room,
kitchen,
bedroom,
cradle, chifforobe,
figures of saints,
a bed with its headboard
and someone there,
you,
slowly sitting up,
an empty space at your side
while, in the air,
the I-can't-say-more
or I've gone mute.
And the thunder, the tempest,
the lightning flashes,
all that electric charge,
mere
background
which rhymes with profound.

Igual que una lanza,
su nítido zumbido:
pasa,
estás en tu casa.

Something like a whizzing
spear:
rest your bones,
come in, you're home.

Celda

Insistes
en mover montañas
bajo el manto
y a las faldas
de una opacidad
franqueable
ni por equivocación,
donde nadie se asoma,
donde la magnolia se ofrece
y además huele
de modo tal que
lo que se abra sean
candados de poros y párpados
y se escuche entonces
algo propio,
un alarido,
una llama
tras los biombos.

Cell

You insist
on moving mountains
under the mantle
and to the skirts
of an opacity
insurmountable
by equivocation,
where no one appears,
where the magnolia offers itself
and also gives off
so much scent,
the padlocks on our pores and eyelids
open
and something strange
comes clear,
a howl,
a blaze
behind the screen.

Visión

Venus de cristal al construirse,
de porcelana al destruirse,
resplandor entre índigo y cobalto
emergiendo de un mar
picado.
Del ojo del huracán,
no del interior de una gran concha.
Mientras la locura
de invocaciones
de tantos mortales
se desmenuza
entre las sales,
en el agua transparente
de un oleaje
Pacífico.

Frente a una fidedigna
figura de cal
sobrepuesta
en un volumen
concebible,
aunque incierto,
yo encarnaba el relato
de cualquier cronología.
Confundida con la marea,
era un solo ir y venir,
un cabo suelto.
¿Me llamaba o yo a ella?
¿Me conmovía o se movía conmigo?
Algo primigenio
insólito
bárbaro
me selló el oído
con un soplo,
un suspiro.

Vision

A crystalline Venus taking shape,
a porcelain one coming apart,
a splendor between indigo and cobalt
emerging from the choppy
sea.
From the eye of a hurricane,
not from inside a great conch.
And the madness
of the incantations
of so many mortals
clears up
with a dose of salt
flicked into the transparent water
of a Pacific
wave.

Face to face with a familiar
whitewashed figure
standing over
a conceivable
but uncertain
depth,
I embodied the tale
from whatever chronology.
Confused in the surging tide,
I was simply coming and going,
a loose end.
Did she call me or I her?
Was I moved by her or she by me?
Something primordial,
weird
peculiar
sealed my ear
with a breath,
a sigh.

Una mancha

Que había que borrar las huellas,
no dejar rastro,
me imponían.

Con toda la fuerza del espíritu,
con retórica de sangre.

Sobre la cama,
un vestido de Primera Comunión
de sencillez monjil,
un velo que hasta el último pespunte
contenía un hasta entonces
sordo
mudo.
Aún las sandalias
gozaban
de un albor
in
mundo.

Colgado del canto de la puerta,
el traje de novia
empobrecido por el color perla
de un futuro
de artificios
comunes y corrientes.

Camisas de fuerza
que a la postre
habrían de mostrar
la lividez
de un camino inverso
a las moradas de lo real,

A Mark

So I brushed away the tracks,
leave no trace,
they told me.

With the force of the holy spirit,
the rhetoric of blood.

On the bed,
an austere
First Communion dress,
a veil designed, to its last backstitch,
to cover an up-to-then
deaf
mute.
Even the sandals
seemed to take pleasure
in their un
clean
whiteness.

Hung from the edge of the door,
my wedding dress
impoverished by the pearly color
of a future
filled with common, everyday
lies.

Durable clothes
that in the end
would show
all the wear
of taking the road in the wrong direction
to the house of the real,

la mismidad atónita
in
maculada.

᠂᠊᠊᠊

Con acentos de gaita herida
de bolsa amniótica vacía
hecha fuelle
que acaece
de pasión rabiosa.

᠂᠊᠊᠊

Entre y ante propios y ajenos,
entre personas que dicen mucho
y no *me* dicen nada,
entre una oreja y otra,
regurgitan
modos de crecer,
de soslayarse,
sobre todo,
ese modo individual,
el fuero interno.

a startled,
im
maculate
selfsame place.

～

With the whoof of a wounded bagpipe,
an empty amniotic sac,
a bellows
stuffed
with a maniacal passion.

～

Between and before the familiar and the foreign,
among people jabbering all night
who tell *me* nothing, who,
between one of my ears and the other,
regurgitate
the acceptable ways to grow up
and evade
above all
my own way,
my conscience.

Colas

Nadie atiende a la conmoción profunda
de los mares
pues en la cresta airada de las olas
apenas si desfilan las espumas
cual zorrillos nocturnos, cola en alto,
contoneándose cual si fueran pavos reales
con el abanico abierto,
no un gran dios
sin pensamiento que lo adorne
o aspire a hacerlo incomprensible.

Grandísimo lienzo abstracto,
que calcina y ahoga por igual.
Fondo de tantos océanos
con aliento y pulso propios:
alguien se yergue,
arrogante,
sin otra cosa que lucir que sus sentidos,
mientras las aguas y su furia,
mientras la tierra y su contención de fuego,
mientras los tornasoles de la cola del quetzal
o el armadillo . . .

Tails

Nobody bothers with the enormous commotion
of the seas
since on the angry crests of the waves
the foam seems little more than a phalanx
of skunks at night, tails held high,
strutting peacock-
like with their fans spread,
not some great
and thoughtless god who embellishes
or aspires to devise the incomprehensible.

A stupendous abstract canvas,
it scorches and drowns equally well.
The depths of such oceans
roll with our own breath and pulse:
someone gets up,
arrogant,
with only intuition to light the way,
while the waters and their fury,
while the earth and its fiery contentions,
while the iridescence of the tail of the quetzal
or the armadillo . . .

Atormentada

Caían enormes sólidos
desde no sé qué alturas,
no sé qué lugares.
Temblaba,
y en la boca
un sabor a tinta. En su punto.

Granizo, quizás,
granos de hielo enormes;
su descenso,
aquel impacto escandaloso,
no me enterró, aterrada,
entre las cobijas.
No fue, no era eso.

Una temperatura bajo cero
circulaba por el centro tierno de mis huesos.
Un verdadero calor frío.

Nada de monstruos a la vista.
Nada de distancias interminables.
Nada de acontecimientos brutales.
Sólo una tormenta de bellotas.
Sólo un ciclo que se cumple
cada cierto número de años
y torna al bosque tropical
un encinar en coro.

Es el miedo.

Tormented

Enormous solids were falling
from who knows what heights,
who knows what places.
I trembled,
and in my mouth
an inky taste. Ready.

Hail, maybe,
enormous kernels of ice;
coming down,
with a scandalous impact,
didn't bury me, terrorized,
under the covers.
It didn't happen, it wasn't that.

A below-zero temperature
drove into the soft center of my bones.
A truly searing cold.

Nothing to do with monsters came to pass.
Nothing to do with endless distance.
Nothing to do with brutalities.
Only the agony of acorns.
Only a cycle that completes itself
every few years
and transforms into a tropical forest
a choiring oak grove.

Which is my terror.

Año Uno * Conejo
Año Luz * Liebre

Quien ha escuchado
el gemido, el lamento,
el aullido
de dolor
quizás de muerte
de un animal,
ha absorbido
la belleza, esa blancura,
la suavidad, esa presteza,
sollozando:

> *herido, un conejo*
> *eleva un grito*
> *y ese grito*
> *distrae mi pensamiento.*

Al instante,
de mí emana
un azoro agradecido,
capaz de bordar,
algún párrafo tatuar
que lo comprenda:

> *te recuerdo como a un conejito*
> *desprovisto de su natural abrigo níveo,*
> *más blando aún*
> *con la carne expuesta,*
> *tu pálida sinparidad,*
> *abandonada a los dardos*
> *de mi amor*
> *que permanecerán por siempre*
> *entre tus músculos y entrañas,*
> *un infalible aguijonear.*

First Year: Rabbit
Light Year: Hare

Anyone who hears
the whine, the lament,
the yowl
of pain
of death, let's say,
of an animal,
has absorbed
beauty, that whiteness,
softness, that quickness,
sobbing:

> *a stricken rabbit*
> *is crying out*
> *and its cry*
> *distracts my thought*

At that instant,
what whelms from me
is a stunning awe
I can no more undo
than if it were tattooed
on my mind:

> *I remember you as a rabbit*
> *shorn of your natural snowy coat*
> *and softer even,*
> *with your flesh exposed,*
> *your unparalleled paleness,*
> *vulnerable to the arrows*
> *of my love*
> *which are fixed*
> *in your muscles, your viscera,*
> *a relentless goad.*

No caíste en una trampa
al ir saltando
entre los campos y praderas
de tu tiempo concedido.

Ningún azar de cazador furtivo
te sorprendió escondido entre hojas secas
clavándote un punzón,
metiéndote una bala,
sin más remedio desangrando
tu propósito ulterior.

Yo fui quien te observó a conciencia
y te causó esa herida incandescente
sin ningún derramamiento.
Esta aflicción no es muerte
ni su causa.
Es liebre dormida entre fulgores
dentro de un conejo ausente,
lista para brincar
inadvertida.
De noche, acaso.
Resguardada bajo el manto
de su espejo.

Bounding across
the fields, the meadows
of your given days,
you never tripped the trap.

No cunning, lucky hunter
took you by surprise in the dry leaves,
running you through with a stick,
piercing you with a bullet
so that hopelessly you bled out
your most covert intentions.

It was I who watched you so intently
and inflicted that luminous wound
without spilling your blood.
What you've got isn't a case of death
or even its cause.
There's nothing there but a hare
asleep in the radiant absence of a rabbit
ready to bolt,
unseen.
At night.
Safe as what pours
from a mirror.

Dulzura

De un clásico manjar
que no empalaga

Rumor esparcido
cuan largo y amplísimo vibra,
confundiéndose
con cualquier otra epidermis,
extensos pastizales,
cada una con su mapa,
su zodíaco.
Anónimo,
esencial.
Inerme
ante amor y muerte.
Que son—ésta, aquél—
laguna o lago
donde el sollo,
el esturión melifluo,
logra en su ascenso
la raya de plata
de un limen etéreo.

Líquida
esmeralda aturquesada,
turquesa esmeraldina.
Este sitio, esa cualquier otra epidermis.
Secuela de algo o alguien,
propia del haber bogado,
navegado de por vida
en saeta estigia.

꩜

Como un disparo,
la cuerda de sutil viola de amor
desentume la emoción
y pulsa:

Sweetness

The sweetness of a classic
confection is never cloying.

As it spreads itself out,
rumor vibrates,
mixing
with the flesh of otherness,
with languorous pastures
each with its own map,
its own zodiac.
Anonymous,
essential.
And defenseless
confronting love and death.
Which are—this, that—
like a lagoon or a lake
where the sturgeon,
sleek bottomfeeder
ascending like
a silver ray,
marks an ethereal threshold.

Liquid
emerald-turquoise
or turquoise-emerald.
This site, that flesh of otherness.
The aftereffect of something or someone
who navigated her life
rowing into the Stygian current
on a clock's arrow hand.

⋰⋰

Like gunshot,
the plucked chord of love's viola
unnumbs emotion
and pulse:

primero,
a la gran deslumbrada por los faros;
sus anclas se sumergirían
en un río de ríos, Ouse,
que pesaría a la larga
más que las piedras
en las bolsas de su abrigo
por parentesco sánscrito,
agua,
de la cual ella no emergería
más que por su madre y lengua,
único oráculo real,
oralidad que mana, rezuma, supura . . .
Dios Santo, en estos borbotones se halla
nuestro primordial sentido, no cabe duda,
descubrió
in situ
la siempre virgen virginal virginia;

luego,
por suerte,
me conduce en salvador retorno
a mi propio Lough Arrow,
mi flecha latino-sud-centro-americana,
Tequesquitengo,
tratando de zafarme de las algas,
ellas inocentes, yo horrorizada,
tragando más y más de las fuentes bautismales
de aquel Tiberiades morelense.
Por fin, los carrizales,
que cincuenta años después reconocería
al clavarme sola, por voluntad,
entre otras ondas, caricias de otros vientos
que me devorarían y devolverían entera,
flotando de muertito.

first,
in the searing beams of the lighthouses,
she would drop anchor
into that river of rivers, the Ouse,
whose Sanskrit roots
came to weigh her down
even more than the rocks
in the pockets of her overcoat,
water,
from which she would only emerge
through her mother and tongue,
a singularly worthwhile oracle
whose orality runs, seeps, spills . . .
Sweet god, in these rising bubbles we trace
our primordial direction, as no doubt
she discovered
in situ
the always virgin virginal Virginia.

later,
by chance,
a salvific journey brought me
back to my own *Lough Arrow,*
my Latin-Southern-Central-American arrow,
Lake Tequesquitengo
where, aghast, I tried to brush off the seaweed,
though it was harmless,
and drink more and more from the baptismal waters
of that Mexican Tiber.
Finally, there were reeds
I would recognize fifty years later
as I dove alone, willingly,
into other waves, freshened by other winds,
that would swallow me but spit me up alive
doing my deadman's float.

El apelativo de aquel otro lago, Flecha,
me mostró sus dos puntas, sus dos ojos
de lanza antigua, de leyenda:
Gae Bolga, única y terrible,
que al adentrarse entre los músculos
se subdividía en múltiples navajas
envenenadas en presente, ponzoñosas en su porvenir,
que sorbían los poderes lentamente.

Así, sólo así,
se moría de amor,
goteando dentro.
Sin más testigo
que esas dos atentas
palabras oculares.

The name of that other lake, *Arrow*,
suggests to me its double-edged point, the two eyelets
of an ancient lance, the legend of
Gae Bolga, a spear so singular and terrible
that as it sliced through muscle
it broke into countless barbs
envenomed in the present,
still poisonous in the future,
sapping what remained of the victim's strength.

Like that, just so,
we once died of love,
hemorrhaging within.
With no other witness,
than those two vigilant
all-seeing words.

Machihembrado

I. CERROJO

Yo no pensaba abrir
tu diario de viaje,
pese a todo,
con la adivinación al centro de la frente
de que hallaría el tesoro.
No una confesión, ningún secreto:
tu caligrafía perfecta.
Y, disueltas en su tinta china,
tus meditaciones,
tu panorámica frescura,
tu ingenuidad línea tras línea,
horizonte tras horizonte (porque los días iban pasando),
el Atlántico entre tus lagrimales caribeños;
tus tribulaciones,
tus recuerdos y angustias
al escuchar las vibraciones del motor,
la rimbombancia de las hélices,
tu saberte a merced del aire, del viento,
tu saber a fondo que a fondo
vivirías ya
en otros,
cada quien con su diario
y con su viaje.
De los míos,
ni hablar.

De sobra celebraste el volar sin alas
tú, el bien nacido,
de impecable pensar, proceder, conversar
y describir con opulencia, sin jamás exagerar;
de sabio hermosear y escorar y embrocar

Tongue-and-grooved

I. LOCK
I hadn't thought to open
your travel journal,
despite everything
with divination on my mind,
in the hope of coming across some treasure.
And there was no confession whatsoever, no secret:
just your perfect handwriting.
And, parsed in India ink,
your meditations,
your panoramic originality,
your unaffectedness line by line,
horizon by horizon (since the days were passing),
the whole Atlantic sloshed between your lachrymal
Caribbeanisms;
your tribulations,
your memories and anxieties
on hearing the mutter of the engine,
the low hum of propellers,
your knowing yourself to be at the mercy of air, wind,
your intimate knowledge of those depths
in which you would go on living
in others,
each with their own journal
and their own journey.
My own
I take for granted.

You took flying without wings to its rapturous limit,
you, the well born,
impeccable in your thinking,
your manners, your conversation
and your opulent descriptions free of hyperbole;
knowing how to charm, to take charge, to reel in,

y embromar y anolar.
De luminoso sonreír con la mirada.
De escuchar sin eco y exclamar
discretos vituperios.

to tease and savor.
You, with your lustrous eyes smiling.
Soaking up the listening,
blaming with discretion.

2. CERRADURA

Otras chapas, broches, aldabones.
Un veliz cubierto de sellos, distintas latitudes,
Holanda, Austria, Canadá,
zuecos, blanca planta alpina,
ánades en plena trayectoria:
lo que te había dado alas,
justo lo que yo quería.
Sabiéndote muerta,
al guardar ahí mi primera ropa de muchacha,
unas medias de nylon que no sabía ponerme,
una falda con forro,
tu retrato,
fetiches, un collar,
me transformaba en ti,
agua de Lourdes evaporada
que no es la santa ni la virgen
pero produce sus milagros.
Sólo visibles
en el ataúd del mundo.

2. LATCH

Various locks, hooks, knockers.
A suitcase plastered with seals, stamps from distant latitudes,
The Netherlands, Austria, Canada,
wooden shoes, white alpine flowers,
mallards in flight:
your own wings spread,
all I could wish for.
With the knowledge of your death,
I've kept my childhood clothes in your suitcase,
those nylons I never knew how to wear,
a silk-lined skirt,
your portrait,
fetishes, a necklace
that changed me into you,
the evaporated water from Lourdes
that, neither saint nor virgin,
can still instigate miracles.
On display only there,
in the coffin of the world.

Sueño de música estelar

Para Beto y sus criaturas

Me dirigí a la ventana,
convocada por fuerzas irresistibles.
Mas no bastaba columbrar la escena desde ahí.
Había que ir al encuentro de una noche
de ópalo esparcido,
pintado con brocha gorda,
desaparecidas las fronteras,
cualquier atisbo de luz eléctrica,
cualquier silueta de casas, granjas,
humanas edificaciones.

Sólo murmuraban las estrellas:
se podía ver su movimiento,
escuchar su diálogo,
y éste
correspondía a fragmentos
que has cantado
y cantarás
hasta el final de los tiempos.

Un timbre personal
en exacta coincidencia
con el movimiento,
la posición, el cambio intergaláctico
de astros nacidos
para que la nota prolongada de una sombra,
a la que se pide consejo,
y la de una nota corta que responde de verdad,
seguida de un silencio necesario,
correspondan de manera natural
a un destello
sin ton ni son,
que hasta ofrezca una figura

Dreaming a Music of the Stars

For Beto and his creatures

Spurred by irresistible forces,
I went to the window.
But nothing came clear from there.
I had to go out under the scattered
opals of a night
painted in thick brushstrokes,
its horizons utterly gone,
no glimmer of electric light,
no silhouettes of houses, farms,
or human structures.

Only the stars murmured:
I could make out their movements,
overhear their conversation
so consonant
with fragments
you have sung
and will keep singing
until time shuts down.

A personal timbre
coinciding precisely
with the progression,
the position, the intergalactic shift
of stars born
so that the protracted note of a shadow
to which we look for guidance,
and the quick note of truth's response
punctuated by a necessary silence,
might naturally correspond
to this glittering,
no rhyme or reason,
although it suggests an image

a los ojos lejanos del intruso
que pide formas, sólo formas,
aunque fuera una silueta
de osas, canes, escorpiones,
seres reconocibles,
incapaces, pobres criaturas,
de abandonarse a la música del cielo,
ese abismal
devanar
de la madeja simple
de espacios
como éste.

to the eyes of whomever
scans the stars for shapes, mere shapes,
even if only the silhouettes
of bears, dogs, scorpions,
familiar animals,
poor, helpless creatures
abandoned to the music of the spheres,
that abysmal
unwinding
of the plain skein
of such spaces
as this.

Los viejos almacenes

Para Alastair y Jane Reid,
por su mapa íntimo

Una casa bautizada,
júbilo por siempre:
"Los viejos almacenes"
algún día contuvieron
campestres aparejos, telas burdas,
ornamentos de Oriente, perfumes;
lo mismo una soga
que un lazo
que una cinta de colores;
lo mismo una cuerda de amarre
que un moño para vestido de encaje
o para adornar la cola de caballo;
lo mismo un rollo de alambre
que una guirnalda.

Hoy aloja imágenes,
libros finamente encuadernados,
personas envueltas en piel más fina aún,
y laberíntica.

Ahí,
toda emoción al ras
se pone al centro de la mesa,
se paladea y se incorpora;
todo acertijo se resuelve.

≈

Quien habla de un "incidente",
a un interlocutor omnipresente
de cuerpo ausente,
si es que entiende
a semejante mente

Those Old Grocery Shops

For Alastair and Jane Reid,
for their intimate map

A christened house
is a joy forever:
"Those old grocery shops"
used to stock
field tackle, coarse cloth,
Chinese doodads, perfumes;
plus ropes
and lariats
and sashes in fabulous colors;
as well as skirts that matched
cords for knotting
a chignon or embellishing a ponytail;
and a spool of wire
or a wreath.

Today they stock images,
books bound in expensive leather
and shoppers in even finer,
exotic skins.

Now,
any scrap of emotion
serves as a centerpiece
to contemplate and savor;
all the riddles are solved.

⤙

Someone blabbing
about "a happening"
to some disembodied, omnipresent
interlocutor
as if soliciting empathy

y mar embravecido,
¿de qué habla en realidad?

Nada entiendo,
cerca estoy de nada ser
porque el verso conversado
se desahoga
al hacerse "asunto".
¿Y si se le agregaran puntos suspensivos
(martillazos sobre el yunque),
además de haberlo ya entrecomillado
(filigranas, rizos de una rubia
melena atolondrada)?
¿Se tratará de un regalo recibido
a la muerte de alguien muy cercano?

Parecía una caja de música;
tan precioso era
su canto dorado.
Y en vez de la canción de cuna
o algún claro de luna,
se escucha dentro
el dulce
     una cosa bella
     es júbilo por siempre.

Y la destinataria, *Margaret*,
la del suceso extraño,
es la misma
que derrama el llanto
sobre dorada arboleda,
Margaret, la niña
de Gerard Manley,
que no entiende por qué el hombre
va por fuerza al infortunio,
por qué sus lágrimas
van preñadas de usufructo.

and a free pass—
and what's really being said?

Nearly nothing myself,
I understand nothing
because what's spoken
goes slack
when it becomes "a topic."
And if I add quotation marks
(hammer blows on an anvil)
after a sprinkling of commas
(filigree, a giddy
long-haired blonde)?
Would it be like receiving a gift
at the funeral of a friend?

Something akin to a music box, perhaps;
adored for
its golden tones.
But instead of a lullaby
or some song about the moon,
you hear that
sweet refrain
    a thing of beauty
    is a joy forever.

And *Margaret*, who accepts this gift
in a strange sequence of events,
is the same child
who was weeping
over Goldengrove,
Margaret, the girl
in Hopkins' poem
who didn't understand why man
was born for blight
or why her tears
were pregnant with meaning.

La primera,
la que sería tu madre,
nada vierte
de su sufrimiento
inadvertido.
La niña lleva un luto
por la tierra,
el otoño, el mundo;
la muchacha
está de luto
y no lo sabe.

La una no ríe,
pese a su radiante infancia;
la otra muere de risa,
pero la encierra bajo candado
de felicidad romántica.
¿Por qué no se lo dijiste a nadie,
y dejaste, sí, tal secreto al desnudo,
tal adivinanza manuscrita,

> . . . *tema para una semana,*
> *risa para un mes,*
> *ocurrencia para siempre?*

Pienso, sobre todo, en la última parte.
En ti, tomando clases de quien sería tu esposo,
y dándole clase a quien resolvería el asunto,
a su vez tu enamorado, regalándote
el canto dorado del canto de plenilunio
de quien siempre alzó la voz del amor
unido a la agonía de un moribundo:
John Keats,
John Reid,
John Duncanson.
Pienso en estos tres
como en agua pasa por mi casa,

The first girl,
the one who becomes your mother,
is never distracted
from her secret
suffering.
She dresses in mourning
for the landscape,
autumn, the world;
she is grieving
and doesn't
know it.

The first girl won't laugh,
despite her radiant childhood;
the other dies of laughter
she keeps locked behind
her sentimental illusions.
Why didn't you tell anyone
or leave, why not, some clue
to your curious secret?

> . . . *an argument lasts a week,*
> *a laugh for a month,*
> *but a prank goes on forever?*

I think, more than anything, about the ending.
There you were, taking classes from the man to be your husband
and teaching him who was really in charge,
he in turn becoming your lover, gifting you
with his golden voice, that moon-filled voice
of someone who could carry the notes of love
into the agony of dying:
John Keats,
John Reid,
John Duncanson.
The three of them pour through me
like water through my house,

y me permito creer
en los cambios de piel
a modo de tapete de seda
para la humanidad entera;
creer que la poesía es encantamiento
que se rompe sólo por conjuro propio
para hacer llover,
para retratar la fragancia
de las rosas en la tilma,
para dar con el aurum non vulgi
y ponérselo delante
a la niña y a la joven Margaret:
para que ya no lloren,
y mejor
sigan jugando
entre presagios.

and I come to believe
we can change our skins
as someone might change a tablecloth
for all humanity;
to believe poetry is an enchantment
yielding only for a real spell
to make it rain,
to stir up the fragrance
of the roses that brushed a poncho,
to recover the true gold, the *non vulgi,*
and lay it down before
the girl and the young Margaret:
so they stop weeping
and instead
begin to play again
among the omens.

Contar los hilos

Entre las adoratrices
de aquí y de allá,
las únicas que sí sabían
coser y bordar y trenzar,
porque su labor, "la labor",
tenía fómite infrascrito,
era esencial contar los hilos.

Sus *exempla*, siempre los trabajos de otros
[no faltara más poner sus propios paños,
ropones, casullas, estolas, mantillas
de ensoberbecida muestra]:
pongamos por caso, las hamacas.
Las que a cabo se llevaban de manera literal,
hasta la punta o desde ella y hacia ella
en la prisión: manos encarceladas,
las únicas dignas de acariciar el hilo Oso.
Éstas sí sabían lo que es canela,
lo que es vivir intra muros a la fuerza,
consagradas a mantener en pie al sagrado cuerpo
que ha conocido el mayúsculo desdén,
que ha perdido las delicias de una soledad
en pleno bosque, al borde de algún acantilado,
junto al mar.
Gusanos de seda,
arañas que bordan lo más fino y terso,
falanges que, obligadas a marchar,
despliegan una danza entre sus huellas.

Intento contar los hilos
entre las anacrusas del durmiente.
Desde un pecho que sube y baja,
mientras la central eléctrica
es sopor de la conciencia.

Counting Threads

Of all the nuns
from here and there,
only those who could
sew and embroider, plait and braid—
those whose labor, "the labor,"
was considered infectious, *fomite*—
needed to count threads.

Their *exempla*, always the works of others
[unimaginable to display their own kerchiefs,
baptismal robes, chasubles, stoles, veils,
with pride]:
might include hammocks, for instance.
Those literally made by walking
from one point to another across
their cells: though their hands were incarcerated,
they could finger the thread called *Oso*.
It took its toll on them and they knew
what it meant to be forced to live as shut-ins,
consecrated to propping up the sacred body
that suffered such contempt
that it forgot the sweetness of solitude
in the forest, at the cliff's edge,
near the sea.
Silk worms,
spiders that spin finest and strongest,
phalanxes of women who, obliged to march,
left a pattern of dance steps.

       I try to count the threads
       between each anacrusis of the sleeper
       whose breast rises and falls
       but whose humming core
       is a stuporous conscience.

Poder crear
un capullo que al mecerse
arroje a quien contiene
a los oleajes interiores,
azul cielo, azul rey,
azul añil, de bahía, de estuario,
de golfo, de ensenada . . .

Una rodilla emerge;
nudillos doblados sobre la muñeca;
ojos que se abren tras aquel tejido
de puntos cardinales.
Nace el mundo.
Las arenas,
la pedacería de caracolas,
las lanchas ancladas,
un paisaje adormecido.
Hilos son de Ariadna, la más pura,
de Hipnos, el gemelo de la muerte:
de tiempo acurrucado entre los dos.

Hebras de anacolutos,
redundancias
de labor en demasía, de demasía en la labor,
haciendo de los demás y en ellos
lo previamente en uno elaborado,
como quienes al no enseñarse enseñan
que no hay trabajo de amor perdido,
que tarde o temprano se retribuye y se intuye
todo aquello que en el mejor de los casos se diluye.
Las mismas fibras que cuentan y se cuentan,
se entretejen y destejen,
se sacralizan y con ello se profanan,
al unirse o desunirse
tus pestañas.

To be able to create
a cocoon that, swung in a circle,
might fling its living cargo
into the inner waves,
sky-blue, majestic-blue,
indigo-blue, of bays, estuaries,
gulfs, inlets . . .

    A knee emerges;
    knuckles bent wristward;
    eyes opening into the warp
    of the cardinal points.
    The world is born.
    Sands,
    mountains of crushed shells,
    anchored boats,
    a sleepy landscape.
    These are the threads of Ariadne, the purest,
    of Hypnos, the very twin of death:
    and time is snuggled between them.

Filaments of anacoluthons,
a surfeit of redundancies
of labor, of laborious redundancies,
each thread
an elaboration of the one before,
like those who teach without teaching
that there's no love's labor lost
and sooner or later we are each paid and intuit
everything that even at its best is diluted.
These same fibers that count and are counted,
interwoven and unwoven,
are sacralized and so profaned
in the coupling and uncoupling
of your eyelashes.

Agua helada

Amanece en el paladar, y en la cúpula de la mente permanece pegado el sabor de las palabras regionales, la sal, el estilo de abordar un tema: la verdadera diferencia entre una estrella fugaz, en su calidad de originaria de otro mundo, y su señal gemela, la de mar, que se desliza como niño de ronda o se enrosca uniendo sus puntas al centro, para girar y quedar al revés, montarse en su mismidad y ocultarse a placer, no es lo salado o lo insípido, algo que indica sabor o su ausencia, algo que viaja de uno a otro punto, de una a otra escala portuaria, de un matiz a otro. Escucha lo que se te dice al oído: Tráeme "un vaso de agua helada" que, invariablemente, se hallará en la "nevera". No se trata nada más de quitar la sed. Es algo más, mellizo, hasta siamés. Es un personalísimo modo de ver y expresar el universo que, de pronto, resulta propiedad de todos, moneda en curso, voz popular de cada una de las personas que abrirá su puerta y contestará lo mismo con los mismos gestos, y con ello lo hace a uno ser uno. Qué sería, si no, del placer del provinciano en casa. A sus anchas para acentuar como Dios manda y llamarle al pan pan, para nunca establecer una relación directa entre eso que pedía y saciaba y correspondía, lo dicho y lo recibido, y lo que en otros lados mejor se transpusiera en algo que cae encima como "un balde de agua helada", procedente de las "nieves" metafóricas.

Ice Cold Water

The palate clears, but the flavor of regional words sticks to the roof of the mind, salt, style slapped to theme: the categorical difference between a shooting star, otherworldly as it is, and its oceanic twin, slippery as a child at a playground, contracting its five arms toward its center, twirling, turning around, riding itself and abiding in its secret pleasures, neither bitter nor dour, which would suggest preference or its absence, something that simply goes from here to there, from one port to another, from this to that shade of meaning. Listen carefully to what is whispered in your ear: Bring me "a glass of ice cold water" which, no doubt, will be found in the "icebox." But this request has nothing to do with quenching thirst. It has a twin meaning, maybe Siamese. It's a highly personal way of considering and particularizing a universe that, all of a sudden, belongs to everyone, a currency, the familiar voice of all who open their doors and respond the same way with the same gestures and by so doing come to be themselves. What, otherwise, are a provincial's daily pleasures? At ease speaking the vernacular God mandates and calling a spade a spade, avoiding any direct link between what was requested and served and what truly corresponds, the said and the received. And so what in other places might be called *falling head over heels* is rendered here as "a bucketful of ice cold water," an expression derived from purely metaphoric "snows."

III

Arborescencias

III

Arborescences

Imitatio Christi

Copia al carbón
de una época larguísima
en que un tic tac
que había comenzado en inocencia:
con las rodillas permanentemente ensangrentadas,
sucias e infectadas,
con tesón imaginaba imitar
cierta manera de tomar la pluma fuente,
después la firma,
con tal de no olvidar el susurro
de la puerta deslizante
de aquella alejandrina biblioteca.
Fue un error irse de ahí,
alejarse con las costras
levantadas,
dolorosas.
Por ese aljibe oval
se fueron metiendo
en voz alta
las sagradas escrituras,
por la corteza cutánea
del tronco
único
del árbol de la ciencia,
del árbol genealógico
de follajes siempre verdes.

Imitatio Christi

A carbon copy
of a long epoch,
a tick-tock
that started in innocence:
with its knees permanently swollen,
dirty and infected,
in an effort to imagine imitating
a particular way to hold a fountain pen,
and then the signature,
so the shush
of the sliding door
to the Alexandrine library
might not be forgotten.
It was a mistake to leave that place,
to walk off with suppurating
scabs,
aching.
Through that oval reservoir
they went, their muscular voices
hoisting the Scriptures,
and they skinned the bark
from that extraordinary
trunk
of the tree of knowledge,
of the tree of genealogies,
its foliage ever green.

Güiro

Tu tráquea dentro de la mía
resuena sin definición con desafinación
en quebradas gotas que van cayendo
desde lo que sí tuvo sentido alguna vez
hasta el día de hoy,
por el único camino al alcance,
instrumento de rara madera,
una suerte de palo de lluvia
incrustado en el plexo solar.
No hables por la herida,
no desmontes tu escenario,
no congeles esta escena,
demencia pura
del más claro uso de razón,
condición gloriosa,
tu sentido común,
esparcido entre un desierto de sal
y el crepitar del hielo
como un fuego
inapagable.
Tu tráquea tocada con baqueta
se desdice, se contradice,
se maldice y se retracta,
a ratos agua que fluye,
otros agua estancada
en corvas, axilas, lagrimales.
Pero siempre sulfurosa
y celestial.

Yokel

Inside my trachea your trachea
vibrates inarticulately, tunelessly
drops make their way into streams
from what once made sense
right up to today,
along the one road out,
an instrument of precious wood,
your solar plexus inlaid
with the luck of a rain-stick.
Don't talk through your wound,
don't come down from your scenario,
don't freeze up in this scene,
pure dementia
from the clearest application of reason,
a glorious condition,
your common sense
scattered between a desert of salt
and ice crackling
like an unquenchable fire.
When it is played with a cleaning rod,
your trachea
back-talks itself, contradicts itself,
curses itself and retracts,
sometimes the fluid flows;
at other times, fluid pools
in the sockets of knees, armpits. Lachrymal.
But sulfurous too
and celestial.

Allée Marie Laurent

A Mali, por su vida

Soy recuerdo de enramada,
tal vez de arbusto.
En cambio tú seguirás siendo
una mujer que emerge
a diario
desde sus cavilaciones,
cubriendo su solidez de roble
con un velo de seda
pegado a la piel.
Lo demás, lo que uno creería
fronda fresca de fresno
es vestido al aire
que parte de aquel velo y del cabello
que de tan fuerte el aire
cubre el rostro y la silueta,
las uñas de los pies pintadas
de quien no ha salido aún de sí
ni lo hará, pues es lo que es.

Las gaviotas en pleno tráfico y fárrago,
las gaviotas entre corredores de domingo,
bolsas de basura abiertas sin perro que olisquee,
rejas aherrojadas sin perro que le ladre
a nadie,
y luz sobre los edificios
tan increíblemente bellos,
tan creíblemente antiguos,
y la gente
inmersa en tradiciones,
ahí donde, de noche,

Allée Marie Laurent

To Mali, for her life

I'm all memory of branches,
or brambles.
Whereas you
keep emerging
day by day
from your deliberations,
covering your oaky solidity
with that silken veil
you pin to your skin.
The rest, as you, the freshest
frond of the ash tree, suspect,
is a windblown dress
which matches the veil and hair
the wind so forcefully swipes
across the face and profile,
and the polished toenails
of someone who keeps to herself
and will continue to, being who she is.

🖋

A farrago of seagulls, heavy traffic,
seagulls above the Sunday joggers,
trash-bags torn open but not a single dog sniffing around,
rusty gates and no dogs barking
at anyone,
and light is bathing buildings
incredibly beautiful,
incredibly old,
and people
soaked in traditions,
there, where at night,

sobre el Sena brillan los fragmentos
de quienes optaron por vivir
o no vivir más
ahí y así.

En la superficie,
    un salto
    en mis cinco sentidos
    hasta el umbral
    de la memoria.

beyond the Seine
shimmers what remains
of those who chose to live
or not to live
there and so.

From ground-level,
  a leap
of the five senses
towards memory's
threshold.

Poet's Afterword

Ethereal Slipknot: The Intangible Integrity of the Poetic Word

(On winning the Villaurrutia Prize)

One of the characteristics that differentiates human beings from the denizens of other realms is that endless pondering on the meaning of life which leads, in many cases, to warning signs and indications that anticipate, define, even claim to explain signal moments in the journey. I think one marker of writers is the capacity to see, in our childhood and adolescence, harbingers of what we will be and do in the future. My own life was blazed by linguistic epiphanies: first, Spanish-American; later Mexican Spanish, particularly the dialect of the Yucatan; and finally, the classic speech of Mexico City.

In the 1950s, in the Colonia del Valle, we used an everyday lexicon only understood there, one derived from the southeast where my father was from. But in our house, any grammatical inaccuracy, even a small one or a peculiar usage, was considered unforgivable. At some time, I remember picking up from my schoolmates the phrase "I promise to you" as a substitute for "I swear to you," and I suffered the consequences. On another occasion, I casually recommended that a classmate "slurp" a lozenge: her perplexed stare jolted me into that other world where you're supposed to call things by their formal names and sound like a foreigner, if not a complete alien; where you have to call bread *bread* and wine *wine*, although you might be talking about sappy things with friends, for example. Consequently, I breathed in a passion for speaking precisely and a horror for the incorrect and for the morally prohibited bad words.

From there it was a short leap to the silent discovery of the *power* that all this implied, not only by the virtues of connotation but in the sentiments communicable through subtleties: complete proper names as opposed to nicknames or pet names; a sure sense of when to use formal and informal address; and above all, the thousand and one circumstances in which a hidden meaning would exfoliate into multiple meanings. Calling a hairpin "an invisible," a festival ticket "an un-transmittable," a sequence of words "an oration," was risky unless it had something to do with saying prayers.

The said and written in this language and in no other: the world, its infrastructure, the stratosphere, the sublime: all is conceived and experienced through the lens of the word. Before me stood an entity not unlike a person, someone who ruled a micro- and macro-cosmos, who exuded a loving reciprocity and who punished doubters with an awe-inducing expressive clumsiness. In Ramón López Velarde's poem "Sweet Homeland," I was most moved, even in childhood, by the allusions to linguistic intimacy: the "language of love" that offers "the prick of sesame" to cite a sensual reference; the suggestion of "a white man's idiom" which reoriented me towards a geographic reality stronger than any entelechy or religious stricture; López Velarde's afflicted youth who goes underground pursuing something as incomprehensible as a latitude; a line like "the dried-apple cadavers / of birds that speak our own tongue."[1] Without this reference to the reality of words, the reality of the spirit would be inconceivable. Poets are concerned with a known secret, an absolute truth. Czeslaw Milosz, seeing his own language suffer the abuse of those who used it for speculative ends, dared to speak directly to the word itself:

> Faithful mother tongue,
> I have been serving you.
> Every night, I used to set before you little bowls of colors
> so you could have your birch, your cricket, your finch
> as preserved in my memory.[2]

Prey to a strictly argumentative dialogue, Milosz, the exiled intellectual, takes out his shimmering pain, reproaching himself for letting it be used as fodder for "the debased who hate themselves even more than they hate other nations," calling his own language "the tongue of informants, the tongue of the confused." As Milosz's poem goes on, the words begin to clabber in his mouth with each claim made on them, leaving a bitter taste. And at last, the old poet asks for forgiveness and realizes, "Faithful mother tongue, perhaps after everything, it's me who has to save you." The Polish Nobel winner has left scattered in his work incalculable truths that might be summarized in just one: *love your mother tongue until you die.* That phrase, which isn't so magical and doesn't earn any place in posterity, alchemically satisfies our need for "order, rhythm, form, three words that stand against chaos and nothingness."

In retrospect, now I see why, in my poem "The Death of the Kiss,"[3] I was dealt such a devastating response, these syllables that trumped my arrogance:

> Already you've understood,
> you've stretched toward yourself,
> even just a little;
> welcome to the paradise
> of perfect omissions,
> to shadings dissolved in. . . .

All that ellipsis could do was to open the way to a question that continues to gnaw at me:

> Who do you kiss,
> who do you touch,
> to whom are you joined
> gift of fire,
> ethereal slipknot?

FROM MYSTERY TO ETHEREAL CLARITY, ETC.

There I was, from childhood, armed with nothing but words against so many enigmas. In the center of the house of mirrors of this world. Learning to pray helps at such a time. My mother often prayed into our ears, my little brother and me, something that later I discovered wasn't a prayer like "Hail Mary" or "Our Father" but a sonnet by Friar Miguel de Guevara, "To Christ Crucified": "My God doesn't move me to love you or the heavens you've promised me. . . ." It wasn't the image of Jesus wounded that impressed me—that part seemed like a lie—but the peculiar syntax, the sound, the perfectly interlaced syllables of "even though what I wait for won't wait."

Later, victim to an acute religiosity, during the preparatory exercises for my first communion, I remember opening up and telling the confessor, "When I pray, I talk to God, but He doesn't talk to me." For which he advised me, "Pray in *your own words*." This directive gave birth to my first poems and, with them, a whole new *imago mundi*; a capacity to describe perceptions and emotions in a fresh way, with intimate verbs. Of course, those early poems ended up in the trash; their pure and decanted fervor was nothing other than what Helen Vendler calls "Admirable Sentiments in a forgettable language." What I lacked was that form of possession that comes only after you live in literature for a long time and in poetry in particular. As far as this goes, I've chiseled in my depths the burning words of Francisco Cervantes, from his poem "Neither Proud nor Humble":

Give me, Lord, piety for myself
And may my deeds repay you.
I don't expect comprehension from anyone
Because the human machine is limited
And there's nothing else
Other than the alien equilibrium I detest
And which likewise detests me.
Don't think I don't know myself,
But before slipping back into the darkness
You might possibly express yourself by giving me expression.
If that's how it goes, Lord, that's what I'm doing.

My adolescence threw me into a regular reclusiveness, thanks to which I proved you could save the *right words* just to talk with yourself, without the Most Holy watching over your shoulder. I started, then, a dialogue with my personal penumbra. The background music, the accompaniment to this whole epoch, was reading—and the swarm of voices that emerged. I came, in stages, to hear Charles Dickens, Wilkie Collins, Walt Whitman, W. B. Yeats, authors from whom I discovered that when one reads something worth remembering, a human voice is freed. Then the voice of Emily Dickinson became a necessity—if not an addiction; those little poems expanded inside me. Consequently, I began to write in order to speak back to those to whom I'd listened, and to leave vibrating in the air of my defenselessness, a real "fireball voice, / a voice bawling fire."[4] Here's a recent example of mine, an

Echo
In memoriam Emily Dickinson

It would not sound so deep
Were it a Firmamental Product—
Airs no Oceans keep—

Afloat between your lens
and your gaze,
the last consideration to go
across my gray matter
and its salubrious
deliquescence
is
whether or not I'll swim,
whether I'll be able to breathe,
whether I'll live as before.

I'm caught in the bubble
of your breath.
It locks me in.
Drives me mad.

Confined to speak alone,
I talk and listen,
question and answer *myself*.
I hum, I think I sing,
I breathe in, breathe in and don't explode.
I'm no one.

Behind the wall
of hydrogen and oxygen,
very clear, almost illuminated,
you allow me to think
that *the Root of the Wind is Water*
and the atmosphere
smells of salt and microbes and intimacy.

And in that instant comes
the *low echo*
of a *beyond* beyond,
a language archaic and soaked
in syllables and accents suited
for re-de-trans-forming,

giving light,
giving birth to
the melanin
hidden within another skin:
the *hollow* of a voice
which speaks alone.

Thanks not to the writer but to the poem, the trapped instant becomes
an eternity, the newly awakened meanings travel from the world of their
normal use into metaphorical space. Villaurrutia would refer to "the ex-
pression of both the union and indifference of life and death." And I might
only emphasize with italics my own sense of that *indifference*.

WHO LIVES!

Watchword, my shibboleth, defines itself in ascending or descending steps;
one footprint on a strange journey designed like an ouroboros. I'd love
to be able to pin it down with the kind of play that made José Gorostiza
famous: Knock knock. Who's there? The devil. . . . No. Whoever it is,
whoever is on the other side is someone who no longer aspires to possess,
some day, the weight of the persuasive voice among the multiplicity of
informants' voices; someone who no longer needs to express a particular
personality, but who would rather escape personality, flying on drafts of
significant emotions and not on the confessions of the poet. All this is
simply desire. A desire similar to the transformative power of poetry. W. H.
Auden famously wrote that "poetry makes nothing happen," and it's true
that poetry doesn't, for instance, make it rain. But Auden never tired of
writing it. I do think that art is capable of transforming perception. After
seeing a landscape by Turner, our relationship with nature is forever al-
tered. After hearing Seamus Heaney's "The Rain Stick," our ears are more
alert—"like a pipe / Being played by water"—to the miracles of our senses
thanks, in part, to his alliteration. The change is sensed in the certainty
that *the poem is speaking to me*, even though it is not. I would have liked
to have taken the skeptical Auden to one of the Hispanic philology classes
of Dr. Juan Manuel Lope Blanch just to see his face when the professor
asked: "Tell me, class: who rains?"

If poetry teaches something, it is a belief in the marvelous linguistic
world, that archaically defined system of interlacing sounds, that "thing

consumed, thing completed, which exists in itself and for itself, a thing made of language not anecdotes or autobiographical details," as Salvador Elizondo put it. *Watchword* includes a poem of mourning for my parents in which what matters least is the depicted absence of those two figures. What matters more are the sounds that open our eyes:

[oh, voice,
yes, you are sinking nearer, signifying
more and more each time,
searching only to find
yourself at the center of a kind
of immense catafalque, you,
a mummy unwrapped,

a mummy so vividly defleshed and exposed.]

I've come to dream that Xavier Villaurrutia knows what I'm talking about.

Notes
1. From "Cuauhtémoc," by Ramón López Velarde, translated by Margaret Sayers Peden.
2. From "Faithful Mother Tongue," by Czeslaw Milosz, translated by Scott Horton.
3. Translated by Forrest Gander in *No Shelter: Selected Poems of Pura López Colomé*.
4. Translated from Xavier Villaurrutia's "Nocturno en que nada se oye."

Acknowledgments

The author gratefully acknowledges the John Simon Guggenheim Memorial Foundation for a fellowship in 2009 and United States Artists for a Rockefeller Fellowship in 2008.

The translator would like to thank the editors of the following magazines for first publishing these translations.

American Poetry Review, February/March 2009, Elizabeth Scanlon, ed.: "And the Intrepid Anthurium" and "Imitatio Christi"

Cavalier, Fall 2009, Christina Yu, ed.: "The Old Grocery"

Cerise Press: A Journal of Literature, Art, and Culture, Summer 2009, Karen Rigby, Fiona Sze-Lorrain, and Sally Molini, eds.: "Tibuchina Flower"

Columbia: A Journal, Spring 2009, Justin Boening, ed.: "Cell" and "Vision,"

Critical Quarterly, Fall 2009, Ben Lerner, ed.: "Tongue-and-grooved," and "Come on in"

The Fiend, Fall 2010, Andrew O'Donnell, ed.: "Deep Wound," "Almond," and "Dehiscent, Enraptured Invention"

Make: a Chicago Literary Magazine, Spring 2009, Joel Craig, ed.: "What a Din" with an interview conducted by Jen Hofer

Nimrod, Spring 2009, Francine Ringold, ed.: "Who Are You; What"

Poetry, April 2009, Christian Wiman, ed.: "Echo" with an essay on its translation

Poetry, April 2008, Christian Wiman, ed.: "Tormented" with an essay on its translation

Translator's Notes

In my preface I have incorporated three phrases, slightly altered; one from Michel Leiris and one from each of the two manuscript readers for Wesleyan University Press.

In "Who Are You; What?" I have used the Robert Hass translation of Issa's poem for the epigraph.

In "Tibuchina," *meninges* are the membranes enveloping the brain and spinal cord.

In "Maybe Borneo," I have used Seamus Heaney's translation of Dante's lines for the epigraph.

In "My Life's Portrait," *Te Deum* refers to a hymn often sung at the public ceremony in Mexico when, at fifteen, a girl comes of age.

In "First Year: Rabbit / Light Year: Hare," the first four italicized lines are from "The Man and the Echo" by W. B. Yeats (but line-broken aberrantly).

In "Those Old Grocery Shops," *aurum non vulgi* refers to "uncommon gold," a medieval alchemical figuration.

Toward the end of "Ethereal Slipknot," the author mentions José Gorostiza, a great Mexican poet and author of *Death without End*.

Pura López Colomé was born in Mexico City in 1952. She studied literature at the Universidad Nacional Autónoma de México, publishing literary criticism, poems, and translations in a regular column for the newspaper *Unomásuno*. She is the Villaurrutia Prize–winning author of several important books, including *El sueño del cazador*, *Aurora*, *Intemperie*, as well as a volume of collected poems, *Música inaudita* (Eds. Verdehalago, 2004). She is also the translator into Spanish of works by Samuel Beckett, H.D., Seamus Heaney, William Carlos Williams, Gertrude Stein, and others. In 2010, she was awarded the Linda Gaboriau Literary Translation Award.

Forrest Gander is the Adele Kellenberg Seaver Professor of Literary Arts and Comparative Literature at Brown University. He is the author of the novel *As a Friend* and numerous poetry collections, most recently *Core Samples from the World* (2011), and is also an established translator of Spanish-language poetry.